Praise for *The Impost*

'Kate turns the imposter syndror
phenomenon not a lasting condition and that you are not the only
one feeling it. She provides easy to follow real examples to reframe
and manage how you feel, giving you the courage and confidence to
succeed.'

**Nigel Daly, Lead for Leadership, Culture
and Strategy, Ministry of Justice**

'Kate Atkin beautifully weaves research and storytelling, sound theory
and practical advice. *The Imposter Phenomenon* can help you lead a
more successful, happier, and more authentic life.'

Tal Ben-Shahar, author, *The Pursuit of Perfect*

'Such an important topic, brilliantly explained. Let's face it we're all
just making things up as we go along! This insightful book will help
you silence your inner critic and live more courageously. We're all a
work in progress, but you're already enough as you are.'

Dr Mark Williamson, CEO, Action for Happiness

'Kate Atkin knows more about the imposter phenomenon than pretty
much anyone else. She integrates major theories and develops her own
insights into a painful state of being that leaves many of us cringing
when we should be shining. This is a book for anyone who has ever felt
they lacked the courage to be themselves.'

**Dr Roger Bretherton, Chartered Psychologist,
Senior Fellow, University of Lincoln**

'*The Imposter Phenomenon* is a brilliant and accessible read that bal-
ances academic insight with real-life experiences. The personal stories
make it deeply relatable, showing just how common imposter feelings are, while the practical recommendations feel achievable and

grounded in everyday reality. From small interventions to shift your inner voice to finding the courage to step forward with confidence, the book offers tools that anyone can use. Whether you experience the imposter phenomenon yourself or manage people who do, this is an invaluable resource for understanding, supporting and overcoming imposter feelings. A great personal and professional development guide for today's workforce.'

Lindsay Scott, co-founder, House of PMO

'This book has pearls of wisdom in each chapter. It is accessible to all who read it, and everyone will find themes and things that they identify with from a personal or professional perspective. It will definitely give you some "aha" moments!'

Karen Bloomfield, former Head of Talent and Leadership Development, NHS

The Imposter Phenomenon

Pearson

At Pearson, we have a simple mission: to help people make more of their lives through learning.

We combine innovative learning technology with trusted content and educational expertise to provide engaging and effective learning experiences that serve people wherever and whenever they are learning.

From classroom to boardroom, our curriculum materials, digital learning tools and testing programmes help to educate millions of people worldwide – more than any other private enterprise.

Every day our work helps learning flourish, and wherever learning flourishes, so do people.

To learn more, please visit us at **www.pearson.com**

The Imposter Phenomenon

Why you feel like a fraud and what you can do about it

Dr Kate Atkin

Pearson

Harlow, England • London • New York • Boston • San Francisco • Toronto • Sydney
Dubai • Singapore • Hong Kong • Tokyo • Seoul • Taipei • New Delhi
Cape Town • São Paulo • Mexico City • Madrid • Amsterdam • Munich • Paris • Milan

PEARSON EDUCATION LIMITED
KAO Two
KAO Park
Harlow CM17 9NA
United Kingdom
Tel: +44 (0)1279 623623
Web: www.pearson.com

First edition published 2025 (print and electronic)
© Pearson Education Limited 2025 (print and electronic)

ISBN: 978-1-292-46906-5 (print)
          978-1-292-73712-6 (ePub)

British Library Cataloguing-in-Publication Data
A catalogue record for the print edition is available from the British Library

Library of Congress Cataloging-in-Publication Data
A catalog record for the print edition is available from the Library of Congress

10 9 8 7 6 5 4 3 2 1
29 28 27 26 25

Cover design by Two Associates

Print edition typeset in 10/14 pt Charter ITC Pro by Straive
Printed in the UK by Bell and Bain Ltd, Glasgow

NOTE THAT ANY PAGE CROSS REFERENCES REFER TO THE PRINT EDITION

This book is dedicated to my research participants, without whom there would have been no research, and to Obi, my teenage rescue Springer Spaniel, without whom it would have been written six months earlier.

Contents

About the author

———

Speaking to audiences about courage, confidence and the imposter phenomenon, Dr Kate Atkin inspires others to overcome their inner fears. This is Kate's third and most personal book having experienced the phenomenon for much of her life.

Coming from a farming background in Lincolnshire, she was the shy one of three girls. Defying expectations and despite feeling like an imposter, Kate completed an MSc in Applied Positive Psychology in 2015 and in 2024 she received her PhD for research in the imposter phenomenon, coping strategies and psychological courage.

Working with major corporates, universities, charities and the NHS, Kate is on a mission to explain what the imposter phenomenon is, and what it isn't, to help individuals and organisations overcome the impact of feeling like an imposter.

Kate maintains her own website **www.kateatkin.com**

Author's acknowledgements

———

My thanks go to the friends who reviewed this book in draft form with their supportive suggestions and to my editor, Eloise Cook, for her faith in me and encouragement with the early drafts. Thank you also to the whole team at Pearson for doing such an excellent job of bringing this book into the world.

I will be forever grateful to my participants for sharing their thoughts, fears and insights with me with such candour; I am deeply indebted to all 21 of you. Without the unwavering support from my supervisors and their guidance over the years, I would have given up: thank you does not seem enough, but it is all I have. And, finally, thank you to my husband for his constant support and encouragement.

This book is not perfect, but it is written.
I hope you and others benefit from reading it.

Kate

Introduction

'A lot of the time, I think I'm winging it. I think, you know,
this is not technical knowledge, this is common sense.'

Ellie, research participant

Have you ever felt like you don't belong, that you're not good enough
or that you'll be found out as a 'fraud' at some point, even though
you have a track record of success? Or perhaps you would like to go
for promotion or get involved in a different project at work but think
that you are not ready or that you don't have the right skills despite
being encouraged by others. Or maybe you are an expert in your
area but don't use your expertise to speak up in meetings because
you feel that you don't belong in the meeting or worry about looking
stupid. These are some of the feelings and behaviours associated
with the imposter syndrome or, more accurately, imposter
phenomenon. Although imposter syndrome is the more commonly
used term, technically, these feelings should not be medicalised as
a syndrome, so I will use the more accurate term of phenomenon
during the book.

It is important to understand that imposter feelings differ from a lack of confidence. The difference is illustrated by this quote attributed to Henry Ford:

'Whether you think you can, or think you can't, you are right.'

For many years, I found Ford's quote inspirational. It helped me build my confidence, it helped me push my boundaries and it inspired me to change my mindset and think more positively. However, in 2013, when I came across the concept of the imposter phenomenon, I had to rethink. I realised that Henry Ford might be wrong, as not everyone who 'thinks they can' is right. Imposter-style thinking also means that there are people who 'think they can't', but they most definitely can.

This book focuses on the imposter phenomenon, in particular when experienced at work. But that does not mean imposter feelings are restricted to the work environment. Indeed, people have told me that they have felt like an imposter as a parent, a friend, in community roles such as football coach or when part of a volunteer group – and these are just a few examples. In this book, you will find an outline of who experiences imposter feelings and some indications as to why that might be the case, as well as some coping strategies and how you can support others.

Contrary to what many social media blogs and articles would have you believe, the imposter phenomenon is not a women's issue. You may take comfort from the fact that it is a widely experienced feeling by men and women (academic research has been completed in binary categories; at the time of going to print, there is no known non-binary research specifically on the imposter phenomenon). Nor is there a magic wand, a quick fix or fairy dust that I can sprinkle to remove your imposter thoughts. But you can do something about them, you can help yourself and also help others who may be experiencing imposter thoughts.

Imposter thoughts and feelings are, however, not something people generally like to talk about. Can you imagine going to your boss at work and saying that you don't feel you deserve to be in the job you're doing? Or going up to a colleague and telling them that you feel like a fraud and are unsure whether you can complete the project you are working on? People who feel like an imposter tend to keep their thoughts and feelings to themselves, and research with medical students indicates that people may work extra hard to ensure they don't get found out.[1]

If this sounds familiar, then this book is designed to help you. Part 1 offers a greater understanding of the imposter phenomenon, why it's not a syndrome, an indication of who experiences it and potential reasons why, as well as some of the issues that imposter feelings can cause at work. Part 2 covers what you can do to help yourself overcome your imposter feelings and how to cultivate courage. Part 3 suggests what managers and leaders can do to support those who experience the imposter phenomenon.

If these imposter feelings sound like those of someone you work with, then reading this book may enable you to help them. Ironically, telling someone how amazing they are at their job and how much faith you have in them can make their imposter feelings even worse. If you are specifically interested in the role a manager or leader can play, skip to Part 3.

Some people tell me that they like to keep their imposter feelings, saying it motivates them to work hard, to do better and to keep learning. However, the stress and anxiety that often accompany feeling like an imposter are the main reasons I would encourage anyone to take another look at themselves to see whether they really want to continue feeling that stressed. It is highly unlikely that reducing your imposter feelings will decrease your motivation or reduce the standard of your work, but it will reduce your stress levels.

This book is designed to be more of a workbook than a novel. Don't feel that you have to start at the beginning and keep going until the end. Pick the parts and chapters that resonate with you. Read, reread and take time to process what you read. Note down your reflections if that works for you. There are occasional boxes with prompts to encourage you to do this. I have called these 'time in' boxes rather than 'time out' boxes, a phrase I have borrowed with permission from the author and researcher Tal Ben-Shahar,[2] as they prompt you to spend time with yourself and to reflect on your thoughts and actions.

Throughout the process of reading and reflecting, please be kind to yourself. For some people, the imposter feelings go deep, and kindness matters. I also encourage you to maintain a curious mindset. Hopefully, being curious will help you understand your own, and/or others', imposter feelings, why you might feel the way you do, what you can do to rethink your view of yourself and how you can accept how good you really are.

Why am I writing this book?

So, why am I writing this book? Since starting work in my early twenties, and even before then in my teenage years, I have had a feeling of anxiety linked to a fear of not being good enough. I have been fearful of making mistakes and concerned about being told off, anxious that any successes were flukes and worried that, at some point, I would be exposed as a fraud or an imposter – although I did not have the language to name these fears until recently.

These fears started around the time I was 10 years old. In the 1970s, the 11-plus exam was something all children in England sat to assess whether they were academic (in my mind = clever) or practical (in my mind = not clever). The academic children went to high-status grammar schools, and the practical children went to the local secondary schools. My older and younger sisters passed the exam and attended the local grammar school. I failed and went to the local secondary school. This early failure stayed with me as a sense of 'not being good enough'. University was never an aspiration, nor was it encouraged by my school or family. I did complete a Higher National Diploma (HND) at Norwich City College, but I took to heart the joke that HND stands for 'Has No Degree'.

My first career was with a UK high-street bank. During my time there, I constantly felt as if I was just one step away from being 'found out'. Having joined the bank as an office junior at the age of 20, I was quickly promoted onto an accelerated training scheme.

That meant a change of job roles about every six to twelve months and a requirement to take the professional banking exams. While I passed many of the exams on the first attempt, it is the failures I remember. I failed the accountancy module three times, finally passing on my fourth attempt.

Moving jobs within the bank was also challenging. Sometimes, I didn't have any formal training to do the job I had just been promoted to, waiting six months to be trained. But, by then, I had already learnt along the way. The progression of roles was interesting as well as challenging, but it came with a level of stress that I only recognised on reflection. Moving from one place of work to another, it was surely only a matter of time before my mistakes caught up with me. Or so I thought. They never did . . . but does that mean there were no mistakes? Or were the ones I made not significant? Or did nobody bother to tell me about them? Or maybe they haven't been found yet?

Research indicates that people who have progressed in their careers and achieved a level of success that they did not expect are more likely to experience imposter feelings than those who have not achieved such success.[3] Success can, of course, be interpreted in a variety of ways. It doesn't have to be significant promotions or getting to the CEO role in an organisation (though, as an aside, a fear of being found out to be incompetent was the number one fear of CEOs, as identified by Roger Jones in a 2015 *Harvard Business Review* Article).[4] Success can simply be having gone beyond the expectations that others had of you, or that you had of yourself.

As an adult, have you achieved more than your childhood self thought you would? Have you stretched beyond the boundaries of familial or societal expectations that surrounded you when you were growing up? As a farmer's daughter with two sisters, there was the unspoken expectation that one of us would marry a farmer and produce a boy. Sorry Dad, it just didn't work out like that . . .

In 2013 I began a personal and professional journey to do something I never thought I could or would do, especially given my 11-plus failure. Encouraged by my husband, I enrolled at university to study for a master's degree in Positive Psychology. In fact, I began this journey a year earlier, having applied in 2012, but I delayed my studies for 12 months as I thought I didn't know enough. I spent a year reading books on the topic of positive psychology just so I wouldn't show myself up.

So I was in my late forties, when, as a mature student at the University of East London, I chanced across an academic paper titled 'The impostor phenomenon in high achieving women' by Pauline Clance and Suzanne Imes. Reading it, I found myself reflected in much of what Clance and Imes wrote. Their work made such an impression on me that the imposter phenomenon became the focus of my research and, subsequently, incorporated into my speaking work. I progressed to researching how individuals cope with their imposter feelings in the workplace,[5] leading to being awarded a doctorate in 2024 from Anglia Ruskin University in Cambridge.

How did that happen? How can this farmer's daughter from Lincolnshire have reached these academic heights and be running a successful business as a keynote speaker and facilitator of workshops and training courses? Surely I'm going to be rumbled sooner or later. I'm the shy girl who didn't pass the 11-plus exam and wasn't clever enough to go to grammar school.

As you can tell, this has been a personal and professional endeavour. As well as weaving in a little of my own story, this book summarises my PhD research and references research by other academics on the imposter phenomenon. I had the privilege of interviewing 21 people who experience the imposter phenomenon to learn how they cope at work and to understand their thoughts and experiences. They have all been anonymised, and some of their direct quotes have been abridged for clarity and readability.

The following table provides a brief outline of each participant: their pseudonym, age range, sector and job role at the time of the interview. They all experienced either frequent or intense imposter feelings, evidenced by taking the Clance Imposter Phenomenon Scale,[6] and were generous in sharing their experiences and coping strategies with me.

Participant data

Pseudonym	Age	Sector	Role
Amy	40–49	Finance	Automation practice lead
Ben	30–39	Finance	Help desk analyst
Cleo	30–39	Insurance	Insurance policy advisor
Dawn	50–59	Finance	Ex group chief people officer
Ellie	40–49	Insurance	Head of risk
Fay	30–39	Insurance	Chief risk officer
Gail	30–39	Finance	Learning analyst
Holly	50–59	Insurance	Chief information security officer
Iris	30–39	Insurance	Learning & development manager
Jean	50–59	Insurance	Head of marketing
Kelly	30–39	Insurance	Head of client services
Lisa	30–39	Finance	Associate director
Mark	50–59	Insurance	Insurance broker
Nina	40–49	Insurance	Senior risk consultant
Olivia	30–39	Insurance	Managing director
Pat	50–59	Insurance	Head of human resources
Quinn	40–49	Insurance	Human resources business partner
Roger	40–49	Insurance	Marketing & communications
Simeon	50–59	Finance	Head of risk
Tina	30–39	Finance	Digital marketing manager
Una	40–49	Finance	Team manager

My aim is that, based on my and others' researched evidence, I can provide you with some practical ideas that will enable you to reduce your own imposter feelings. Or, if you don't experience these feelings, that it will help you understand more about the imposter phenomenon so you can support others who do feel this way. It is also my hope that this book and my research may help shape or inform organisational policy by increasing awareness of why people who are successful and confident at work on the outside may feel like a fraud on the inside and worry that they will be found out.

Over the years, I have tried to follow my own advice and I'm pleased to say that I am finally accepting that I'm not a fraud, that I do know what I'm doing, that I'm not perfect, but I'm not about to be found out. Hopefully, this book will help you along that path too.

I trust you will find it an enjoyable and worthwhile read.

part 1

—

Understanding the imposter phenomenon, the impact of feeling like an imposter and why it matters in the workplace

chapter 1

What is the imposter phenomenon? And why it's not a syndrome

'In order that people may be happy in their work, these three things are needed: they must be fit for it; they must not do too much of it; and they must have a sense of success in it – not a doubtful sense, such as needs some testimony of others for its confirmation, but a sure sense, or rather knowledge, that so much work has been done well, and fruitfully done, whatever the world may say or think about it.'

John Ruskin, *The Crown of Wild Olive*

Our inner thoughts can motivate us to move forward in life, but they can also hold us back, they can inspire us to achieve our goals, and they can create anxiety. We all have an inner dialogue which, at times, can be positive and, at other times, negative. Our inner dialogue can also create a sure sense of success or a doubtful sense, as referred to by John Ruskin in the chapter opening quote. In the 1970s, two American psychologists, Dr Pauline Clance and Dr Suzanne Imes at Georgia State University, noticed that some of the women they worked with, including post-doctoral and highly acclaimed students, were experiencing negative inner thoughts. They were expressing a doubtful sense of success, which led them to describe themselves as feeling phoney, like an 'imposter'.[1]

Clance and Imes sought to find out what led to these thoughts, especially given that the external evidence clearly illustrated that these women were bright and capable. Their academic paper titled 'The imposter phenomenon in high achieving women', published in 1978, was the first to use the term 'imposter phenomenon'. Their research focused on the experiences of female undergraduate students, graduates and post-graduates, as well as a small number of professional women working in a variety of different fields. What Clance and Imes observed in 1978 strongly resonated with me when I read their paper in 2014 while doing my master's degree.

Even though there was plenty of external evidence to show that these women were capable and academically skilled and that their qualifications and exam results proved they were intelligent, they reported that they did not feel successful on the inside. As Clance and Imes explained: 'Success for women is contraindicated by societal expectations and their own internalized self-evaluations.'[2] In other words, neither the women in Clance and Imes's sample nor society at large expected that they would or should be successful. When success was achieved and recognised by others, the women reported feeling a sense of phoniness, insecurity and worry about being found out as a fraud. Hence Clance and Imes coined the term 'imposter phenomenon' to describe this sense of phoniness and fear of being found out.

The inner dialogue of someone who experiences the imposter phenomenon has a particular tone. It is not only self-deprecating but also admonishes and criticises the self. It seeks excuses to dismiss any positive feedback that does not align with the negative self-view, and it can be stressful to live with.

If you have not experienced imposter thoughts yourself, it can be very hard to comprehend the inner dialogue of those who have; if the external evidence is there, why not believe it? To help you understand these inner thoughts, you'll find a few quotes from my research participants in the following box. If you have experienced imposter thoughts yourself, you may find that some of these resonate with you.

Simeon: 'It's less stressful to feel I'm really good at a job that is below my capabilities. So, in that sense, actually, I'm better than the job I do. But . . . I'm scared of pushing my luck.'

Holly: 'You only ever see the outsides of others. Colleagues appear to be so organised and clever and sophisticated and, in your life, everything is always a bit of a mess.'

Ellie: 'I've had good feedback from my manager but I'm thinking "you're new in post, so how do you know how I should be performing?"'

Lisa: '[My managers say] "you know what you're doing", blah, blah, blah. And you believe all that, but you also think "well, actually, I don't believe that; it's probably got something more to do with money or whatever".'

Iris: 'I really value modesty and not kind of bigging myself up. I don't feel comfortable doing that. But, at the same time, I do like to have recognition for what I've contributed. So, I guess it's an inner conflict that plays out.'

Kelly: '"Why on earth would you want me to be an after-dinner speaker? They must be crackers!" And I thought, well, there's other reasons, budgetary as well – I was cheap. I didn't cost anything and I thought it must be that.'

Throughout the book, I use more quotes from my research participants to give you a greater understanding of the inner dialogue and
thinking of people who experience the imposter phenomenon. By
hearing from others, my hope is that you will be inspired to stop
playing it safe and become more comfortable owning your successes,
accepting the positive feedback, and see the opportunities that come
your way as rightly deserved. But, first, I encourage you to take a
moment to reflect on the statements from the box above.

Time in

- What, if anything, surprised you about these imposter thoughts?
- Which thoughts resonated with you?
- What thoughts of your own would you add to the list?
- How did you feel when reading the list?
- Did it feel like they were inside your head?

You may have felt a little exposed and 'found out'. Or you might be
feeling vulnerable as you reflect on your own imposter thinking.

Remember to be kind to yourself.

It's a phenomenon, not a syndrome

By choosing the word phenomenon to describe imposter feelings,
Clance and Imes made the point that these feelings occur at particular moments in time. For some people, this is at work, perhaps only in
certain meetings or around specific individuals. For others, as mentioned earlier, these feelings occur outside work, maybe as a parent,
a friend, or in relationships. While feeling like an imposter can, at

times, cause high levels of stress and anxiety,[3] these feelings are not the same as a diagnosable mental health condition, which is implied by the word syndrome. Researchers mainly use imposter phenomenon, while imposter syndrome is more common in everyday life. Syndrome may also have become popular because it is much easier to spell than phenomenon; it has fewer syllables and is also far easier to say (as an aside: if you know the Muppet song 'Manah Manah' you will be able to say the word phenomenon with no trouble!). The term 'imposter syndrome' was also popularised by Sheryl Sandberg in her book *Lean In*,[4] and Michelle Obama talks about her experiences of imposter syndrome in her memoir *Becoming*.[5] However, it is useful to know that imposter feelings are not pathological so, throughout this book, I will use the more accurate term phenomenon.

As well as the difference between using the term phenomenon or syndrome, there is a subtle difference in whether we 'suffer from' or 'experience' imposter thoughts and feelings. If we are careful in the language we use, we can have more control over our imposter thoughts and feelings. The phrase 'suffer from' implies that nothing can be done about these thoughts and feelings. By replacing 'suffer from' with 'experience' we gain more control over our thoughts and feelings. That is why I refer to experiencing the imposter phenomenon.

Isn't it just self-doubt?

There are countless times that I hear people refer to imposter thoughts when what they are really talking about is self-doubt. Saying 'I suffer from imposter syndrome' has become very popular and, sometimes, appears to be worn almost as a badge of honour. At a leadership conference I attended in 2023, several people spoke from the stage about their imposter syndrome, recounting a time when they started a new job or attained a promotion. While there could be some imposter thoughts in those situations, usually what the person is describing is the normal, inevitable self-doubt that is felt when in a new situation, be it a new project, a new team or a new job.

One interesting conversation I had on the difference between imposter feelings and self-doubt was with someone who had recently got her first job in the UK after completing her PhD in India. Preena (not her real name) grew up in India, studied at university there and had recently moved to the UK. She had felt very confident during her academic studies and knew her PhD subject inside out. But, when I spoke to her shortly after she had started work, she described feeling lost and said she was having a crisis of confidence, wondering where all her positive, confident feelings had gone. During our conversation I suggested that her feelings of self-doubt were completely normal, and the look of relief on her face was palpable. She had thought she was 'suffering' from 'imposter syndrome'. Through our discussions, she realised that the feelings she was experiencing were resulting from starting a new job in a new country and were not, in fact, imposter feelings. This was normal self-doubt because she was in an unfamiliar environment. Preena realised that her track record of success and her confidence lay in her academic studies, not in the workplace – yet. That confidence will come in time, with experience.

Imposter feelings can look and feel very similar to self-doubt, but there is a distinct difference between imposter-style self-doubt and normal self-doubt. Self-doubt has been described as a 'state of worry and rumination'[6] and is particularly prevalent in new situations where there is no previous experience of success. Experiencing self-doubt can be beneficial when you are doing something for the first, second or third time. It can prevent arrogance, hubris and unnecessary risk-taking. It can also aid preparation and encourage careful diligence for the task at hand. But, if self-doubt, worry and rumination continue for the fourth, fourteenth or even fortieth time, despite previous successes, then it is likely to have developed into imposter-style self-doubt.

Time in

Take a moment to think about a time when you experienced self-doubt:

- What was the situation?
- Was it justified?
- Were you new to the situation or experience?
- Or did you already have a track record of success?
- Was that experience of self-doubt beneficial? If so, in what way?

On reflection, do you now think it was imposter-style self-doubt or normal self-doubt?

How do you feel about that situation now?

It's not a lack of confidence

As well as self-doubt, imposter feelings are also often confused with a lack of self-confidence. Indeed, some researchers have found a link between low levels of confidence and high imposter feelings.[7] This suggests that, as confidence grows, imposter feelings should lessen. However, although one piece of research[8] indicates this happens, it isn't the case for everyone. Some people have a sense of being confident in the task at hand but still feel like an imposter.

When you find yourself doubting your knowledge, skills or capabilities, is it really a lack of confidence? It could be, especially if the situation or task is one you haven't faced before. But, if you have a track record of success, it is more likely to be imposter-style thinking where evidence of previous successes has been excused or attributed to external factors.

Self-confidence was termed 'self-efficacy' by Albert Bandura in 1977; he defined it as 'the perceived ability to succeed at a given task'.[9] As suggested in the previous paragraph, confidence grows through positive, successful experiences, creating a track record of success. When you lack self-confidence and worry about whether you can do something, those feelings can be helpful to ensure you don't over-estimate your knowledge, skills or ability. This is especially true if you don't have the relevant experience or a track record of success. As your experience grows, so does your knowledge, your skills and your ability. Yet, we don't always recognise and internalise that growth.

During one of my workshops on confidence, a participant expressed surprise at Bandura's definition of confidence being so task-specific. She was hoping to increase her self-confidence so she felt confident all the time. However, self-confidence is not an all-encompassing umbrella. Imagine if you were to feel confident all the time, even when trying out something new; there could be some surprising consequences and some major risk-taking! Overconfidence could mean that you don't spend time preparing for a presentation, believing you can 'wing it' even though you don't have the experience. Or maybe you don't check the financial figures of a project or bother to keep an eye on the budget, as you have confidence that it will all be ok in the end. These are exaggerated examples, but they illustrate the importance of a dose of normal, healthy self-doubt and, where a lack of confidence is appropriate, justified and beneficial.

In contrast, imposter-style self-doubt appears when you put your successes down to external factors such as luck, being in the right place at the right time or thinking that people are just being kind to you. Such as believing you were offered a job because the interviewers liked you. This was the thinking recounted to me by one lady who was new in post when I was giving a talk at her company's premises in London. She was convinced she only got the job because the interviewers liked her, not because she was the best candidate. Or perhaps you put your successes down to the fact that someone has made a mistake. This was certainly the case when I received a distinction for my first ever academic essay (but I didn't dare ask the university to re-mark it!).

If it is not luck, then maybe success is just the result of hard work. Some people put their successes down to effort rather than ability, experience or skill. After all, 'anyone can do well if they work hard', 'it's nothing special'. If successes are attributed solely to hard work by those experiencing the imposter phenomenon, they may conclude that they must keep working hard to avoid being discovered as an imposter. In this situation, imposter feelings lead to a tendency to overwork, perhaps spending evenings catching up on emails or taking hours to prepare for meetings. This tendency to overwork also comes with the danger of burning out.

If you attribute success to hard work, luck, or both, you are forgetting that knowledge, skills and abilities are just as important. If there is a recipe for success, I suggest it would include a sprinkling of luck, a sprinkling of hard work and three big dollops of knowledge, skills and abilities.

Stop ruminating

Spending time planning and preparing for future events can be helpful, as can reflecting on lessons learnt from past events. But, when rumination caused by self-doubt becomes excessive, it is unhelpful and leans towards creating anxiety. Ellie, one of my research participants, says her mum keeps reminding her to keep her head in the present and not overthink situations.

Catching your inner chatter and stopping rumination before it spirals out of control can be difficult. One helpful strategy is to talk about your inner thoughts with someone else, such as a mentor, as this provides you with an external perspective (more on this in Chapters 6 and 7). Another strategy to prevent rumination is to write down your thoughts. I was advised to do this after returning from a week-long leadership training course while working for Barclays Bank plc. I had been one of just two female leaders in over one hundred attendees and was one of the youngest, so felt very out of place. Externalising your thoughts onto paper can stop them from running round and round in your head.

James Pennebaker's research in this area[10] indicates that expressive writing, such as writing about how you are feeling, can catch the negative thoughts and associated negative feelings and help prevent them from spiralling out of control. But it doesn't work for everyone. I once heard Pennebaker recount a story of a caller to a radio show where he was the interviewee. The caller said she'd been practising expressive writing for more than 12 months and challenged Pennebaker on the fact that it didn't work. 'Why didn't you stop?' he asked. The key to stopping rumination is to select something that does work for you. Try out several different strategies, stop doing those you don't like, and stop if you don't find them useful. That applies to all the tips and strategies in this book too.

If you notice that you tend to ruminate, perhaps it is also time to practice self-compassion.[11] As someone who has personally experienced severe imposter thoughts over many years, I can attest to how unkind we can be to ourselves inside our heads. We are often our own worst enemies and would not say such harsh things aloud to another person. If we practise kindness, curiosity and compassion towards ourselves, research indicates that this can reduce imposter feelings and ease the stress and anxiety they cause.[12] Chapter 7 provides more suggestions on how to do this.

Building confidence

While this book focuses on the imposter phenomenon, I am taking a little diversion here to suggest some ways that you might like to use to give your confidence a boost. A lack of confidence and imposter feelings are not one and the same but, as mentioned earlier, they are often confused. Building your confidence when doing something new requires different strategies from those needed to overcome imposter feelings.

Sometimes, putting on a confident pose by standing tall or sitting upright can help boost your confidence.[13] Taking a 'fake it until you make it' approach is often proposed as an effective way to boost your confidence in the moment and can work well. However, as I cover in Chapter 7, it doesn't work for imposter feelings. In online meetings, looking at the camera rather than the faces on the screen can create an impression of confidence, whether you feel it or not. To others in the meeting, you appear to be looking directly at them. Whether online or in-person, sitting upright in meetings indicates you are engaged. Sitting back might be comfortable and be your thinking pose, but you may appear disinterested or withdrawn.

Research suggests that reframing a feeling of nervousness to one of excitement creates a different thought pattern, which can reduce nervousness.[14] While this strategy worked for many of those taking part in that research, it doesn't work for everyone. I can remember trying to tell myself I was excited before doing my first (and only) five-minute stand-up comedy routine. I was pacing up and down outside the room before my turn to go on stage. I was telling myself how 'excited' I was about the opportunity, only to ditch the attempted excited reframe and revert to using a bold body posture on stage to fake my self-confidence.

Perhaps acknowledging nerves, as well as saying you are excited, might be useful for you. Being 'nervacited' is perhaps more truthful to the experience of a lack of confidence and embodies a mix of nervousness and excitement. 'Nervacited' is a word made up by the daughter of one of my workshop participants. Her daughter uses it whenever she is trying out something new. As her mother explained, her daughter decided to meld the two words together to describe her feelings more accurately. Sometimes it takes a seven-year-old to instil wisdom into adults . . .

Another strategy to boost your confidence is to take time to reflect on your past positive experiences. Or perhaps you prefer to seek an encouraging nudge from someone who knows and supports you, referred to by academics as 'social persuasion'. Or maybe vicarious experiences give you encouragement to stretch your comfort zones. This may come from seeing people do the things you want to do or achieving the things you want to achieve, and you take encouragement by thinking: 'Well, if they can . . . I can.'

As I mentioned earlier, self-doubt is part of both imposter feelings and a lack of confidence; it is the imposter-style self-doubt that is unhelpful and can be detrimental to experience. But, when you are doing something for the first time, a feeling of self-doubt, alongside a lack of confidence, is normal. Interestingly, you can feel confident and be experienced in a situation or task, yet paradoxically you may still worry about being found out or whether it will go well. And, if it doesn't go well, your internal imposter thoughts may tell you that this one failure means that all the other successes you have achieved were flukes.

Time in

Think of a couple of situations where you would like to have more confidence and a couple where you already feel confident. Take some time to replay those situations in your head and write down your thoughts relating to each situation. What are you telling yourself?

Now take some time to review these thoughts objectively.

- How do you feel as you do this?
- Which are imposter-style thoughts, and which are normal self-doubt?

How can you reword your imposter thoughts?

Reframe imposter syndrome to imposter phenomenon. It is not a mental health condition or something you suffer from. It is something you, or others, may experience at specific points in time, either to an intense or a lesser degree. And change 'suffer from' to 'experience'; your thoughts are not you.

Self-doubt occurs when you lack confidence and when you feel like an imposter. The key difference is in the external evidence. Normal, healthy self-doubt occurs when you are doing something for the first, second or, perhaps, third time. Imposter-style self-doubt occurs when you already have a track record of success. Recognising the difference can help reframe the feelings.

A lack of confidence is not the same as feeling like an imposter. When building your confidence by stretching your comfort zone and feeling nervous, try rewording your feelings to being 'nervacited'.

chapter 2

What does the research say?

'Being extraordinary does not necessarily mean obtaining a position of honour or glory or even of becoming successful in other people's eyes. It means being true to self. It means pursuing our full potential.'

Quinn and Quinn (2002) p. 35[1]

When in conversation with others about the imposter phenomenon, several questions come up time and time again: Is it a gendered issue? Why do women experience it more than men? (They don't.) Where does it come from? Is it linked to our personality? This chapter answers these and other questions based on existing research into the phenomenon.

Early thinking among academic researchers was that women were more affected by imposter feelings than men. But this does not seem to be the case. Subsequent research has found that men and women experience the imposter phenomenon in roughly equal proportions.[2] So, contrary to what social media might have you believe, imposter feelings are not more prevalent in women than men. Even though the initial identification of the imposter phenomenon by Pauline Clance and Suzanne Imes was inspired by the feelings and behaviours they observed in women, they acknowledged that the feelings were also likely to be experienced by men.[3]

When speaking to a mixed audience, men will often approach me afterwards and describe their experiences of feeling like an imposter. They generally tell me that they assume their imposter feelings are also felt by others: 'If I feel like this, then surely others will too.' However, women tend to tell me that they assume they are the only ones with these intense feelings of phoniness: 'It must be me; I'm weird . . .'

Who does it affect?

Imposter feelings are prevalent in so many people, but it is a feeling that we generally don't like to talk about. Many people hide their inner doubts and insecurities, even from their closest work colleagues. After all, there is the fear of what they might think of you if they knew.

One of the privileges I have is facilitating conversations on the imposter phenomenon through my workshops, research and talks. It is lovely to hear feedback from people as they begin to share their imposter thoughts. Some people say they feel 'relieved' by sharing their imposter feelings and realise that they are 'not alone'. Others feel 'vulnerable' and 'emotional'. Sometimes it feels 'cathartic', which came from an NHS surgeon nearing retirement who spoke about his imposter feelings with others for the first time in his career. Occasionally, talking about imposter thoughts feels 'embarrassing' or 'silly'. This is because verbalising inner thoughts allows an objective look at the thinking and may create a realisation that the inner thinking is not as accurate as first thought. But, whatever the emotion, a sense of connection is created through these discussions when someone realises that these are feelings that many people experience, not just them.

We now know that many people do feel like an imposter, possibly more than you might think. In a talk in 2007 at Columbia University, John Gravois quoted 1980s research by Gail Matthews and Pauline Clance, which mentioned that 70 per cent of people felt like an imposter at some point during their career.[4] If the figure is to be believed, it leaves 30 per cent of people who won't experience imposter feelings.

A few of that 30 per cent may overestimate their capabilities, known as the Dunning–Kruger effect. This is where a person's sense of confidence comes from ignorance – they are unaware that they lack knowledge or capability. Instead, they believe they are capable in a specific situation, even when there is no evidence to support that belief. Psychologists Justin Kruger and David Dunning from Cornell University found that participants from four separate studies who scored in the bottom quartile on tests of humour, grammar and logic significantly overestimated their performance and ability.[5] Kruger and Dunning surmise that it was their lack of self-awareness that prevented these people from recognising their own shortcomings. In the workplace, an example might be someone who avoids attending training courses, believing themselves already to be knowledgeable, or someone who overpromises on a task, having overestimated their ability to complete it.

Some of the 30 per cent may find it hard to understand why people who are perfectly capable at their jobs and have the evidence to prove it, don't accept their own capabilities. If you can see the external evidence that someone is doing a good job, and often not just good but exceptional, it can be difficult to comprehend why that person does not accept the praise for their work that is heaped upon them. Especially if you've not experienced imposter feelings.

If you are lucky enough to have never felt like an imposter, the statistics indicate that there is a high chance that you will be working with someone who does. If you are privileged to have an open conversation about their inner fears, please do not express surprise at their feelings or tell them how great they are in an effort to reassure them. That can make the feelings even worse. Instead, listen to them and seek to understand their point of view. You will find more on supporting people with imposter thinking in Chapter 9.

Do men and women respond to their imposter feelings differently?

While current research indicates that men and women report experiencing imposter feelings approximately equally,[6] what they do when they experience imposter feelings may be different. Whether this is solely down to gender is arguable, as societal expectations and upbringing may also influence responses and reactions when experiencing the imposter phenomenon. Imposter thoughts can be influenced by whether we expect to be successful or not. The intensity of imposter feelings can depend on how someone reacts to the outcome of a task, particularly if it is successful, and the causes that they attribute that outcome to. Men and women appear to react differently here, particularly when the outcome is successful. In their 1978 article, Clance and Imes observed that women tended to put their successes down to temporary causes, such as luck or effort. In contrast, men seemed more likely to credit their successes to a stable, internal cause, such as their own ability.[7]

This observation by Clance and Imes is consistent with research by social psychologist Kay Deaux, who found that people were likely to say that an unexpected outcome was just down to luck.[8]

However, if the outcome was expected, people were more likely to attribute it to their own skill or expertise. So, perhaps one of the causes of imposter feelings is whether we expect to be successful or not . . . and that expectation can be of our own making, from our upbringing, from the society we live in, or even the organisation we work in. Indeed, I have had men tell me about their experience of gendered expectations and feeling the societal pressure put on them to succeed at work. Perhaps, generally speaking, men are (still?) brought up to expect to be successful.

Research indicates that self-handicapping behaviour is another way in which men and women may respond differently to potential failures.[9] Self-handicapping is a behavioural or cognitive strategy whereby individuals create obstacles or excuses that allow them to explain potential failures to themselves to maintain their self-esteem. An example of behavioural self-handicapping might be procrastinating by spending time working on small, easy tasks before starting to write that report or going out for the evening for a few beers the night before a big presentation. This allows failures to be rationalised as 'I didn't have enough time' or 'I was very tired'. Research indicates that men are more likely to engage in this type of behavioural self-handicapping than women.[10] Women, on the other hand, are more likely to engage in cognitive self-handicapping.[11] An example of cognitive self-handicapping might be attributing poor outcomes to external causes beyond the individual's direct control, such as not sleeping well or feeling under the weather. Both behavioural and cognitive self-handicapping provide external reasons for failures and are associated with the imposter phenomenon.[12]

Sometimes, observable behaviours such as speaking up or even speaking over someone in a meeting, putting themselves forward for projects or promotions or saying 'I can . . . ' instead of 'I can't . . . ' may be driven by expectations from others or societal conditioning. It is also possible that these observable behaviours, such as the appearance of arrogance or overconfidence, may conceal imposter thoughts. So it's important not to believe everything you see on the outside of others.

Where does it come from?

The triggers and causes for the imposter phenomenon are many and varied. There is no one-size-fits-all reason for the feelings, much as there is no one-size-fits-all solution either. This section covers some of the causes identified by academic research, as well as some of the anecdotal factors I have noticed over the past 10 years. It is not an exhaustive list, but the experiences shared by my research participants may help you identify where your own imposter feelings have come from. They may also help you gain a greater understanding of others' experiences.

Gendered expectations

Early academic thinking[13] in the 1970s and 1980s, was that the imposter phenomenon might be a consequence of women feeling a need to conform to societal expectations, such as the expectation that women are 'homemakers'. Imposter feelings are heightened when someone steps away from the norm and achieves more than society expected or more than their own family expected. Back then, success for women was contraindicated by societal expectations – in other words, society didn't expect women to be successful. So when they were, it was risky or inadvisable to acknowledge the success. Successful women were potentially seen as a threat, less likeable and disruptive.[14] As a result, success was often downplayed or attributed to an external factor. This type of thinking helps to fuel an internal sense of phoniness, thinking you have deceived others and increases the worry that you will be found out to be an imposter.

This observation was made at a time when intelligent women forging their own paths and careers were sometimes seen as challenging traditional 'masculine roles'. For some people, this perception of societal expectations may still hold true. In 2018, while at Ohio State University, Natasha Quadlin[15] manipulated over 2,000 job applications by adjusting the gender of the applicant, their grade and the subject they majored in to assess whether these factors impacted hiring decisions. Quadlin found that women benefitted from being given moderate grades, but high grades reduced the likelihood of them being hired. In another survey, high-achieving men were called back for a second interview much more frequently, at a ratio of 2-to-1, than high-achieving women. That rate increased to 3-to-1 if the major was in maths. Quadlin surmises that gendered stereotypes can penalise women who attain good grades. So even though progress has been made in equality since 1978, for women, sadly, it still may not help your career prospects if you are too clever.

Some of my research participants expressed concerns about societal expectations. They wondered how much these expectations, particularly gendered expectations not just from society but also from their colleagues, friends and even their family, contributed to their imposter feelings. In Fay's experience, it was her friends who compared her career against their own, which Fay found 'very frustrating' when her friends 'don't recognise how senior I am. Because quite often they'll say, "but you don't have children",' implying that she has defied their expectations by progressing in her career and not having children.

Another gendered issue was highlighted by Jean, who says: 'One of the big things that women don't do, in my experience, is ask for pay rises, and I think it is one of the reasons why women earn less than men. Men ask for more money. And I didn't know that until I read about it and thought, "that's me". I've never asked for a pay rise and, when I've been offered a job, I've never negotiated the salary, but men do. And I'm going to change, but it feels utterly unnatural and wrong.' Jean also suggests that 'bossy' is a word reserved for assertive women: 'Women who act like men, super confident, assertive, all that kind of stuff, you're verging on [being labelled] "bossy". That word only gets used for women. It's not used for a bloke. But, when it's a woman who is assertive, society doesn't like it, and women don't like it in women either.'

Another of my participants, Amy, an automation practice lead in a finance organisation, also discussed the gendered aspect of her imposter feelings: 'I think there's still a lack of knowledge of how to effectively incentivise and motivate women who may not be confident 100 per cent of the time.'

So when we butt against societal expectations of how we should act, perhaps women do feel more like an imposter? Confident, self-assured, successful behaviour is still gendered and may not be what society expects from women (yet . . .).

Success

Achieving more at work, such as a higher position or greater responsibility than you ever imagined, can be a reason for imposter thoughts to emerge. One of my workshop participants related how she had progressed quickly in her organisation. She is now in a role where she is working with colleagues who are older and more experienced than she is. To prove to herself that she deserves to be there, she sets unrealistic standards for herself and works long hours. Unsurprisingly, she is feeling stressed and anxious as a result. Another workshop participant said that people often take her for being seven or eight years younger than she really is, which, as she explained, is a significant proportion of her life. This impacts the way she perceives people speak to her. She feels spoken down to and thinks she is seen as less experienced. Consequentially, her imposter feelings increase.

Quinn, another of my research participants who is currently an HR business partner, describes the pressure he feels from himself to progress up the career ladder: 'I can do HRBP level role very comfortably, but it wouldn't be right for me to stay at this level. So I'm looking for a promotion to the next level, because that's the level I need to be at. It doesn't mean some bits aren't going to scare me or I'll think, "oh, perhaps I'm not cut out for this" at times. Those thoughts will go through my head. But it's a duty on all of us not to sit there with an asset that you're not developing or you're not using. That's just wrong or a waste to me.'

Gail also mentioned the expectations relating to her career development: 'You're being told, "think about your career development, where do you want to go next? What do you want to do next?" Hold on a minute, I've only just settled into my role! That makes me nervous; there's much more expectation on me.'

Many people I speak to who experience the imposter phenomenon have, like me, had jobs and careers completely different from those they expected. Tina, also one of my research participants, never planned to be a digital marketing manager – she was going to be a palaeontologist. Another participant, Holly, recounted how her friends and family called her career decisions 'brave and courageous'. Now in her fifties and a chief information security officer, Holly says: 'Doing what people would call a courageous career move isn't that courageous; you still have your home and your family and, you know, the worst thing that can happen is that your career goes down the spout. So courageous doesn't feel like the right word; I was just thinking it's more about doing things that were unexpected.'

Career successes may also be dismissed and explained away. In Iris's example, she wondered whether she was promoted because of her gender rather than believing she was capable or had earned the promotion: 'I've been given promotions without going for them. But that has always led me slightly to being like, you know, but why was that? Was there no one else available? Is it because we need to achieve a quota of females at that level?'

Cleo also wondered why she had achieved her level at work and similarly questioned whether her success was because there was no other candidate for the role: 'Some people think that I'm successful. I don't share that view. I mean, I can see their arguments, that the chances of someone from somewhere else coming and the outsider getting the job; I see why that is quite unlikely. And because I've achieved that, it can be viewed as a success. But I don't feel that way. I feel a proper fraud. I sometimes revisit the process and the steps that have led to this and wonder what happened. Is it because when I applied there wasn't any other candidate? So I was at the right place at the right time and I managed to get it.'

These examples illustrate that rapid or unexpected promotion can cause imposter feelings. Couple this with careers progressing beyond childhood expectations, and you have a good recipe for the imposter phenomenon.

As mentioned in Chapter 1, research indicates that, despite the generalised expectation that success will increase self-confidence, when it comes to imposter feelings, the opposite is the case.[16] Being successful may, in fact, be a reason for feeling like an imposter. Achieving a level of success and attributing the reasons for the success to the fact that you happened to get lucky, you were in the right place at the right time, or that the tasks were easy, can lead you to reason that anyone could do what you do. So when people suggest that what you have achieved is significant, special or extraordinary, you may dismiss that suggestion and feel that they have misunderstood what was involved in the task and how easy it was.

Sometimes, working extra hard on a task means that a successful outcome is attributed to the hard work. In this situation, success is not attributed to luck. Instead, the successful outcome is put down to the fact that you worked hard. As a result, labelling the achievement as a success may seem undeserved. After all, it was 'only' achieved through hard work, not skill or expertise. Or perhaps you are so skilled that little effort is required, and successes come easily, leading you to dismiss the outcomes as nothing notable or special.

Of course, luck and hard work do contribute to success. However, no amount of luck or hard work will make something successful without three vital ingredients: knowledge, skills and ability. Imposter-style thinking forgets these three vital ingredients.

Some people I have had the pleasure of talking to have moved to the UK from Europe or further afield. Travelling to and working in a different country from where they were born is often not what they had planned to do. Going beyond childhood expectations, whether your own, your parents' or society's, can increase imposter feelings. I was the shy sibling, yet I am the one who developed a career as a professional speaker. I was also the one who failed the 11-plus exam and wasn't academic, yet I am the one with a PhD. Olivia describes how her impoverished childhood has driven her to feel that she mustn't waste her potential: 'I know I've got something here of value and I feel it would be a complete waste not to get the most out of that as possible and a lot of that is monetised because I grew up in a household with no money and my parents still have very little income.'

The definition of success in a work context varies from individual to individual. It may include achieving a senior management position in an organisation, earning a salary greater than you imagined, or moving countries to advance your career. Success, in whatever form, especially when unexpected or unplanned, can be a factor in creating imposter feelings.

Time in

- -

- Has your career been as you expected? Or have you 'fast-tracked' or taken a different direction?
- What were you going to do, who were you going to be, when you grew up?
- How is that different from what you are now doing?
- How might that be impacting your imposter feelings?
- How have your knowledge, skills and abilities contributed to your success? (In addition to hard work and luck.)

- -

Perfectionism

A desire for perfection is common in those who feel like an imposter. Nothing short of perfect is good enough. In my talks, I sometimes describe an early childhood event that gets many knowing looks and chuckles of recognition. Consider this scenario: you come home from primary school having achieved 8 out of 10 in a spelling test. When you arrive home feeling pleased with your results, you are immediately asked, 'which two did you get wrong?' While this is a natural question for parents who want to see their child improve, it can land very differently with the child. Thoughts such as 'I'm not good enough', 'I've failed' and even 'I have to be perfect to be loved' may consciously or subconsciously go through your mind, as they did for me. My father could be hypercritical, and my mother had perfectionist tendencies. So working hard and achieving top marks became a way of earning parental love and approval, or so I thought. Translate this into the workplace, and nothing short of perfection is good enough.

This hypercritical parenting style is intended to encourage the child to do their best. Yet, how do we know when our best is done? A 'do your best' mentality can lead to overwork and burnout, both known consequences of imposter feelings.[17] On the flip side, a hyper-supportive parental style can also lead to imposter feelings. I remember meeting a client whose mother had told her she could do anything she wanted and that she would be amazing at whatever she did. Yet when my client failed her first driving test, she was brought down to earth with the realisation that what her mother had told her wasn't true. She wasn't amazing at everything. If she could fail a driving test, she could fail anything, despite what her mother had told her. The fear of failing that she subsequently developed was a factor in her imposter feelings and high levels of perfectionism.

Now, if you are a parent reading this and wondering what you can do to support your own children, you will find that many of the suggested strategies in this book can also be applied to parenting. While not a parent myself, I particularly like two books that you may find useful. These are Carol Dweck's *Mindset*[18] and Philippa Perry's *The Book You Wish Your Parents Had Read (and Your Children Will Be Glad That You Did)*.[19] Both have some good messages about failures, successes and effort. Whether you are a parent or not, I recommend reading them.

I had an insightful conversation with a co-panellist at an imposter phenomenon event who had never experienced imposter feelings. Her insight was that her mother had taught her how to fail and instilled a mindset that failure was a learning opportunity. So maybe celebrating children's failures more than successes might be helpful? I know of a few parents who have made 'failure cakes' on certain occasions for their children and discussed the lessons learnt from the situation. They don't reserve cakes and celebrations just for successes. Celebrating failures in the workplace may be inappropriate, but acknowledging and sharing the lessons learned from failures is important and beneficial.

Other childhood messages

Other childhood messages may impact the development of imposter feelings. Being told, 'don't brag,' 'don't get too big for your boots,' 'pride comes before a fall' and 'nobody likes a smart-arse' can stay with us into adulthood. These messages may lead to success being seen as something to be ashamed of rather than something to feel proud of.

When someone with imposter thoughts has successes at work, their childhood messages may reappear and lead them to downplay those accomplishments. This can result in success feeling undeserved, attained by fluke, or even that someone has made a mistake in recognising the success. This was the case for Fay, who, when I spoke to her, was in her mid-thirties and working as a chief risk officer for an insurance company. Fay talked about an earlier time when she had applied for a new job at a different company. A few days after she was offered the job and had accepted it, she phoned the HR manager to tell them that she was withdrawing because they had made a mistake in selecting her: 'I rang her and said, "I can't do this job, I don't know what I'm doing. You need someone better." And she went, "no, you're going to come, and you're going to do it, and you're going to do it well." And I did!' Thankfully, the HR manager had the insight to recognise Fay's fears and provided support and encouragement rather than accept Fay's withdrawal from the role.

Another participant, Dawn, who was in her fifties and working as an HR director, reflected on her childhood experiences and how they relate to her imposter feelings: 'I've learned by myself that I can actually deal with the issues and pack them away, they're not permanently gone but I can pack them away . . . the experience of going to boarding school at eight actually made me far more resilient than I probably appreciated, even into late adulthood. But I can still be that little girl in that front hall being left behind, dropped off on a Sunday night quite easily, even now. It normally comes when I'm feeling vulnerable and I think people think I'm out of my depth, or I think I'm out of my depth.'

Mark describes how his school years led him to be shy: 'I was brought up in a fairly strict environment, you know, not getting a huge amount of freedom, went to an all-boys school so I had difficulty relating to the opposite sex and I think that's what made me think I was so introverted for many years of my life. It was almost a shyness that was forced upon me.'

One message I was often told as a curious child was, 'don't be nosey.' So even now, I can refrain from asking deeper questions, particularly during casual, social conversations. Or maybe you were once told that you spoke too much or were labelled a chatterbox. From then on you forced yourself to stay quiet, and now you find that you are not sharing your ideas and suggestions. Or perhaps, like Mark, you had the shy label and still find yourself reluctant to enter a room full of people, make presentations or contribute to meetings.

Time in

- -

- What childhood messages can you remember receiving?
- Have you challenged them recently?
- Do they still hold true?

- -

Personality

I am often asked about the link between personality and imposter feelings. There is limited research in this area, but some links have been identified with the personality traits in the *five-factor model*[20] that is used in academic research, although not in the workplace. The five factors are *openness to experience, conscientiousness, extroversion, agreeableness* and *neuroticism*. Academic research[21] has found a correlation between experiencing high imposter feelings and low levels of conscientiousness. This initially appears to be counter-intuitive. Surely individuals experiencing imposter feelings would pay particular attention to their work and, so, be highly conscientious? Whether it is a causal link or just a correlation remains to be investigated, but the researchers suggest that the low reporting on conscientiousness may be due to someone with extreme imposter feelings holding themselves to a high standard.

The researchers also found a link between imposter feelings and neuroticism. Neuroticism, as defined in the five-factor model, is the characteristic of being easily upset, experiencing strong negative emotions and being prone to anxiety and worry. Those with frequent or intense imposter feelings tend to report being more emotionally unstable on the neuroticism scale – not that we like to think of ourselves as neurotic! However, despite a few researchers aiming to classify the imposter phenomenon as a maladaptive personality trait,[22] my view is that the imposter phenomenon is not, in and of itself, a personality trait. Rather, it is an experience of negative thoughts or emotions in certain situations.

The impact of otherness and belonging

Several research articles[23] highlight the impact of otherness and how a lack of belonging increases imposter feelings. Much of this research highlights the sense of otherness and lack of belonging among participants from ethnic minority groups, as well as in women at all stages of their careers in academia.[24]

Many workplaces have equality, diversity and inclusion (EDI) initiatives in place to foster equal opportunities and remove discrimination, as well as processes and policies to increase a sense of inclusion or belonging among employees. However, a sense of otherness or lack of belonging felt by those experiencing the imposter phenomenon may not always stem from one of the nine protected characteristics covered under the Equality Act of 2010 (age, disability, gender reassignment, marital or civil partnership status, pregnancy and maternity, race, religion or belief, sex and sexual orientation),[25] which applies in Great Britain. Imposter feelings may also have another cause. One of the things that participants in my research frequently highlighted was qualifications, a lack thereof, or the wrong sort.

The irony of qualifications is not lost on me. The positive impact of a PhD on my imposter feelings may not just be due to understanding the phenomenon in more detail. It may also partly be down to me accepting that I am knowledgeable on the topic and that I might just belong in academic circles.

For many of my research participants, even though they had the knowledge, skills and experience to do their roles, their imposter feelings were heightened if their qualification was not in the 'right' field, or if they lacked an appropriate qualification, or if their qualification was of a lower level than their colleagues. As a result, they felt as if they didn't belong. The following extracts illustrate some of their thinking about qualifications and the way they compared themselves with others. See if any resonate with you.

Ben, who has five years' experience in an IT support role, said: 'I'm not particularly qualified for the IT industry. I haven't got any formal qualifications.'

Ellie is head of risk at an insurance company. She has over 20 years of experience in risk management, a psychology degree and a master's degree in risk management. However, she still believed her qualifications 'could be a lot stronger' because her master's degree was in healthcare risk management rather than insurance risk management.

Gail is a learning analyst at a financial institution. She explained that she had 'no qualifications. I didn't finish college. I didn't go to university. I do have one business and admin. qualification, but that was just a free course. So, in terms of qualifications, I have absolutely nothing – two GCSEs, I think!'

Cleo, an insurance policy advisor in her thirties, commented: 'It's just easy to feel like a fraud case when, out of all the people you know, I'm the only one who didn't study mathematics.' Although Cleo has a first degree and a master's degree, neither of these were in mathematics.

Lisa, who's in her forties, is an associate director working in the City of London and compares her lack of qualifications to the qualifications that others have: 'Everybody's talking about what university they went to and what degree they've got, and then you're going to have to say, "huh, not me. Just the local comprehensive school!" It doesn't matter that you've been doing the job for 30 years, and they've only been doing it for 5. When you work in the City, they're all such lovely people. It's very rare these days to come across people who are unpleasant, but they're all so well educated.'

In Tina's example, she did her GCSEs and went straight into the workplace and now works as a marketing manager. Two years before we met, she completed a Level 3 qualification in digital marketing, which is equivalent to an A-level qualification. But Tina still compares herself to her team and chuckles wryly, saying: 'In the wider team, I have graduates that have marketing as part of their business degree, for example. And I still compare myself [negatively] to them. Whereas I've done something that purely focused on marketing, they've done a wider degree. I still think that I'm not qualified, but I am!'

Alongside the issue of qualifications as a reason for not belonging, my research participants cited several other ways in which they felt 'other', as if they did not belong in their workplace. Their imposter feelings also increased when there was a lack of role models in the organisation or industry, when they were in meetings with senior colleagues and when they felt the weight of societal expectations, as the following extracts illustrate.

Ben describes how his imposter feelings overpower his courage when at work: 'The imposter overpowers, almost controls the situation and says, "you shouldn't be here, you don't deserve to . . . you've not done anything to actually achieve this".'

Cleo described the impact of not seeing anyone in her industry with the same skill set as her, as well as the impact of being younger than her colleagues, and female: 'There have been lots of meetings where I'm the only female and the only non-white on the call. And it's, it's just very obvious and it doesn't help with fitting in. We have meetings with the CEO, ministers and other quite senior people. I often look like the youngest on the call and of the "wrong" gender.'

Gail works in learning and development and finds that her imposter thoughts can spiral out of control at the simplest of triggers, such as when somebody doesn't respond to an email: 'I think a lot of people know I don't come from a corporate background and that I'm not particularly well educated. So for me, if somebody higher up doesn't respond to emails or doesn't interact with me in a way that I see them interacting with other members of my team, I start to think, is it because I'm not good enough, or I've upset them or they're annoyed at me, that maybe, that they don't think that I deserve to be here. And then I start saying, "well, maybe that's because I don't deserve to be here".'

Holly is in her mid-fifties and is chief information security officer for an insurance company. She doesn't see herself as belonging for two reasons: 'I see myself as quite a clumsy person sometimes, you know, I feel quite awkward often in conversations. I feel I'm not part of the group.' Like Cleo, Holly discusses otherness from the perspective of gender, needing to look as if you belong: 'So there's also the visible look. Having spent many years working in information technology, which is not particularly female but certainly ethnically quite diverse. When I moved into information security it was even less female.'

Nina, a senior risk consultant in her forties, says people tell her that she can be too aggressive or bossy: 'And it's like, maybe you're not telling me that for the right reasons. Maybe it's not that I'm aggressive; it's just that you don't like a woman to tell you what to do.'

For Fay, as chief risk officer, it was societal expectations around parenthood that increased her imposter feelings. She explains: 'There's a societal expectation that, at 36, I should be married and have at least baby number 2 on the way. I sit on an exec. team of five; I am the only woman . . . it's unexpected that it's a woman [on the board].'

Kelly, head of client services in insurance, felt that the gender bias is more unconscious than deliberate: 'Insurance being still so male-dominated does leave you feeling like an outsider some of the time. You know, if you're with a group and they're all laughing and joking. There might be a noticeable change when you enter the group of men who are going to talk about the same things; they're probably not doing it on purpose. It is different being a female in a room full of men, and that can make you think: "Maybe you're not supposed to be here".'

Comments made by other people can unwittingly trigger a sense of otherness and increase imposter feelings. Sometimes, these are half-hearted compliments and, sometimes, they come from those closest to us. At a conference in London, one of the delegates, who works as a contractor, mentioned to me in the break that her mum still asks her: 'When are you going to get a proper job?' Even though she has successfully worked as a contractor for over 30 years!

As human beings we have a desire to be right. We experience confirmation bias,[26] where we discount evidence that does not match our own perceptions and self-beliefs. So our self-perception and the natural desire to maintain the view we hold of ourselves can be another reason we continue to feel like an imposter – even when the external evidence clearly indicates otherwise.

While positive feedback can be really helpful in reducing imposter feelings, the opposite is also true. Counterintuitively, positive feedback can heighten imposter feelings. This is especially true if the receiver does not believe the feedback giver, suspects an ulterior motive, or the feedback is so glowing that it is too far removed from the self-perception. In these cases, it can be very easy to discount the feedback and maintain the self-perception of not being good enough.

Managers may praise team members for work well done, but this can fall on deaf ears. In this example from Ellie, she laughs as she says: 'I've had some really good one-to-ones with my manager, really positive, really, really good feedback. But what plays in my head is that they don't really know . . . '

Failing to update the self-view

As mentioned earlier, imposter feelings were first noticed in highly successful women. Putting gender aside for a moment, one question is: why do *successful* people feel like imposters? When you are successful, when you have achieved something significant, or when you have gained a promotion, your knowledge, skills and experience grow. However, this growth is often not internalised, meaning that the individual has not fully absorbed or recognised their development. We may fail to update our view of ourselves to incorporate our new-found success. It can also seem preferable to downplay successes rather than acknowledge them to ourselves and to the outside world, possibly because of childhood messages where bragging was frowned upon. Yet acknowledging your successes to yourself is not bragging. Knowing what you are good at is not boastful. The successes that each of us achieve can be acknowledged on the inside and worn lightly on the outside.

To assuage our imposter feelings, some people, including me, have sought to gain more knowledge, more learning and more personal development. However, our inner imposter tells us that we should know *everything*. So we then educate ourselves more, work harder, read up on a wider variety of topics and sometimes spend hours doing internet searches to increase our knowledge. But I have grown to realise that *the more I know, the more I realise I don't know*. Perhaps a better insight would be to recognise that we do not *have* to know *everything* to do our jobs well. We will continue to learn, and we can update our self-view to acknowledge what we have already learned. After all, nobody will ever know *everything*.

Time in

- Where and when do you think your imposter feelings started?
- Do any of these examples resonate with your own experience?
- What, if anything, exacerbates your imposter feelings?
- Is your self-view outdated?

Culture and corporate environment

Despite what some social media blogs would have you believe, imposter feelings are not always down to an individual's 'faulty thinking'. Corporate culture and environment can also be responsible for triggering imposter feelings. In 2021, Ruchika Tulshyan and Jodi-Ann Burey published a *Harvard Business Review* article titled 'Stop telling women they have imposter syndrome'.[27] Tulshyan and Burey argue that imposter feelings may be caused by 'systemic racism, classism, xenophobia, and other biases' and they suggest that the 'fix' for imposter syndrome does not lie within the individual. Instead, it is important to 'create an environment that fosters a number of different leadership styles and where diversity of racial, ethnic, and gender identities is viewed as just as professional as the current model'. Although I don't agree with everything in this article, I wholeheartedly agree that corporate culture can be one of the causes in various ways, such as being macho, intellectual, competitive or controlling.

Systemic racism also still exists, and bias of any form can be a trigger for imposter feelings. Faizah Mustafa's research with Black, Asian and Minority Ethnic (BAME) participants[28] supports this. Many of her research participants initially thought they were experiencing the imposter phenomenon but came to realise that racism was the primary reason for their feelings of not belonging.

While organisations can positively impact their staff through values and culture, many of my research participants cited examples where the corporate environment had had a negative impact that increased their imposter feelings. Some of the organisational issues mentioned were the frequency of change programmes, changes in processes, a sense of not knowing enough in a culture where asking questions for clarity or to aid understanding was uncommon, a fear of negative judgement, a feeling that their work was being checked up on resulting in a loss of trust, an unsupportive culture or unsupportive manager and poor leadership styles. That's a long list!

It is important to be aware of the impact that a feeling of not belonging can have on an individual and to understand the real reasons behind their imposter feelings. Their imposter feelings may be an entirely rational response to corporate, organisational, cultural or societal factors outside their control.

Ben, in IT support, says: 'I do struggle with imposter feelings. I've been in the role for two years now. Usually, within 12 months, I've got my feet under the table . . . with this role, it changes so often. It's almost weekly, if not monthly, that we get a new system that we've got to deal with . . . I've never been challenged [by the IT support ticketing process] as much as I have in the last two years. I have to constantly remind myself that it's part of the process. It's the company; if I don't like it, leave.'

Dawn, in her role as HR director reflects: 'It's about asking those idiot questions and that the fact you're asking them means you don't know the answer, when the corporate environment is one where knowing the answer is all that matters.' She says that 'growth comes from your willingness to demonstrate a level of vulnerability.'

Simeon, head of risk, says: 'There's a constant atmosphere of quite personalised judgement, and it gets quite wearing. We pay enormous amounts of lip service to being a happy, team-oriented, collaborative workplace . . . we're not. And it's not just this organisation, it's the industry. You go to another bank, and it's slightly different but, basically, it's the same. Sort of like every day is a prisoner's dilemma.'

Tina, a marketing manager in a financial firm, comments: 'In the industry, there are an interesting bunch of characters . . . some of them are truly horrible, and to do the work for them I know that I don't want to because they're not very nice.'

Fay, as chief risk officer, says: 'Companies have a moral responsibility to be developing climates within their organisations that prevent imposter phenomenon or syndrome spiralling. I definitely took a hit when someone said to me, "you're no good." Stab. Twist. Now, he's been on many leadership programmes; he should have known better.'

Time in

- Are your imposter feelings caused by external factors?
- What impact is the culture in your workplace having on you and your imposter feelings?
- How can you influence the culture in your team?

chapter 3

How do
I know if I 'have'
imposter syndrome?

'I believe that everyone else my age
is an adult, whereas I am merely in
disguise.'

Margaret Atwood, *Cat's Eye*

I am often asked, 'how do I know if I "have" imposter syndrome?' If you have never felt like an imposter, this may surprise you. Surely you would know if you 'have' imposter syndrome? But it is a really common question, possibly because the person is seeking reassurance of some sort. In fact, a more accurate question would be, 'how can you tell whether you are *experiencing* the imposter *phenomenon?*' While it may seem as if semantics are unimportant, the word 'have' suggests suffering and something you can't do much about. In contrast, *experience* and *phenomenon* have more of an association with something that will pass and that you might be able to do something about. Indeed, there are established coping strategies and methods you can put into practice to reduce or even eliminate imposter feelings (these are covered in Chapters 6, 7 and 8).

The language used for imposter feelings is important. As I mentioned in the first chapter, the commonly used term 'syndrome' suggests something medical and pathological and something you 'suffer' from. It implies that the imposter syndrome is something that can be diagnosed. But it isn't a clinical mental health condition, and there isn't a clinical diagnosis. You won't find imposter syndrome, or imposter phenomenon, in the *Diagnostic and Statistical Manual of Mental Disorders*, nor should you. However, it should be noted that frequent and intense imposter feelings can sometimes lead to clinical anxiety and depression.[1]

Imposter thoughts and feelings vary in frequency and intensity depending on the situation. They may also be cyclical, where one moment you find yourself experiencing intense imposter feelings, then the situation changes, the outcome is successful and you feel a sense of relief. You get over your imposter feelings only for them to return perhaps just a short while later, or in a few weeks, or perhaps months. They could be triggered by a similar situation, where you wonder: 'Can I repeat that success? Was it just a fluke?'

By changing your language, you give yourself some power over your imposter feelings. Recently, when I was presenting my research at an academic conference, I nearly forgot to explain the distinction between syndrome and phenomenon. It was only when I was asked a question at the end of my presentation about the difference that I was reminded to cover it. What surprised me was the impact that my last-minute explanation had on the audience. For some people it was their biggest personal 'aha' moment from my presentation. So don't underestimate the impact language can have on empowering you or others to understand and deal with the imposter phenomenon.

What if I really am an imposter?

Another question I am often asked is: 'What if I really am an imposter?' Some people worry that they really are imposters, that they are 'faking it' and will be found out, and that their successes are flukes and have nothing to do with ability. Those experiencing the imposter phenomenon are not actual imposters. A genuine imposter deliberately pretends to be someone else, sometimes with criminal intent.

Perhaps one of the most accomplished genuine imposters is Frank Abagnale Jr, immortalised in the film *Catch Me If You Can*. Among other escapades, Abagnale managed to masquerade as an airline pilot despite having no flying qualifications (thankfully, he did not actually pilot a plane; he only occupied the 'jump seat'). Almost as incredibly, Abagnale also managed to pass himself off as both a doctor and a lawyer. Interestingly, a 2023 *New York Post*[2] investigation discovered that Abagnale may have even been fraudulent about his exploits, having made up or exaggerated some of his tales. Now that is a real imposter!

This extract from Ellie, an enterprise risk manager with a psychology degree working with senior management, indicates how some people think when they worry about whether they are real imposters. During her interview for my research, she described how she prefers to know the minutiae of everything. But she also realises that she can't go into the level of detail that she would like because of the demands of her job. Plus, she is aware that the chief operating officers she works with know their divisions inside out and better than she does. As a result, she starts questioning herself: 'You know, maybe you've got imposter syndrome . . . but what happens if you really are a bit rubbish, and you really can't do what you're doing, and you just put a label on it thinking you can do it, but actually you really can't do it . . . ' Ellie has extensive experience; she has been in risk management for over 20 years and has received lots of good feedback from others. She is not a real imposter. Instead, she is unnecessarily questioning herself.

So the imposter phenomenon is an inner experience, a *feeling* of fraudulence. It is not a conscious, deliberate attempt to defraud, deceive or dupe others. To reiterate, the 'imposter syndrome' is a misnomer. It is not a syndrome, and it does not refer to *being* an imposter.

For those experiencing the imposter phenomenon, the external perception of others is far more positive than their own view of themselves. This is the opposite of individuals whom we might call arrogant or hubristic, where their view of themselves exceeds the view others have of them. (I'll leave you to think of your own examples, but I'm sure you can find one either close to home or in the media spotlight.)

There are a couple of research papers suggesting that some people are 'strategic imposters',[3] where they deliberately deploy false modesty, play down their successes and pretend to be less capable than they truly are. This may be to gain likeability and acceptance from others. While 'strategic imposters' may indeed exist, they are not to be confused with experiencing the imposter phenomenon. Particularly frequent or intense feelings, which can be truly debilitating for the individual.

So, how do you know if you are experiencing imposter feelings?

If you are looking to identify the imposter feelings for yourself, read the statements in the 'imposter statements' box that follows. Depending upon how many resonate with you, and how intensely, they will provide an indication of whether what you are feeling could be the imposter phenomenon. I am being deliberately vague by not creating a set number of statements for you to agree with, or a set scale of intensity, as the imposter phenomenon is not a diagnosable condition (despite what some blog posts may tell you). There are validated questionnaires, used for research purposes, which assess the intensity of the feelings of imposterism on a continuum rather than a straightforward 'yes, you have it' or 'no, you don't'. The most prominent of these questionnaires is the Clance Imposter Phenomenon Scale, which I used for my research.

For an example of a continuum, imagine tasting cheese: a mild cheddar has very little flavour and is unlikely to make you salivate. A medium-strength cheddar has more flavour and may make you salivate. It is tasty and not overwhelming. An extra-strong cheddar will make you salivate and the flavour may be overwhelming for some people (coming from Lincolnshire, I can recommend Lincolnshire Poacher as an excellent example of an extra-strong cheddar).

The continuum is somewhat similar with imposter feelings. Most people will probably experience the 'mild cheddar' variety of imposter feelings at some point. These mild feelings are easy to cope with and likely to pass quickly and are often part of the experience of normal self-doubt. Several people will experience the 'medium-cheddar' feelings. They are uncomfortable, definitely noticeable, but not debilitating. And some people will experience the 'extra-strong cheddar' imposter feelings at certain points in their lives. These feelings are highly uncomfortable and potentially debilitating, triggering anxiety and even depression in some people.[4]

In addition to the intensity of imposter feelings, the frequency of the feelings also needs to be considered. Eating a little extra-strong cheddar occasionally may not be a big deal. But eating a lot of it, say three times a day, might at first seem ok but, in the long term, it is likely to be detrimental to your cholesterol levels and possibly make you feel nauseous too! The same goes for imposter feelings. If you frequently experience the intense, extra-strong cheddar variety of imposter feelings, they are likely to take a toll on your well-being. One of my participants had intense imposter feelings every time she met with her manager, which was weekly. Others said they experienced it daily at work, particularly in meetings.

Here are some statements from my participants showing how their imposter thoughts and consequent anxiety resulted in physical symptoms.

Holly recalled a time when she participated in a highly stressful meeting: 'I realised that I was so anxious and stressed about it that my body temperature had just dropped. Rather than getting hot, my fingers were blue with cold. It was a really weird situation actually to have the physical effects of anxiety so strongly.'

Iris, a learning and development manager, described her imposter feelings in terms of what anxiety feels like to many of us: 'My heart rate is up, and in my stomach feeling fluttery or a bit sick; that kind of sensation.'

Ben, who is in his thirties and works in IT for a large bank, said: 'Basically, it's like it's a panic attack, but it's not always obvious. I could sit next to my partner, parents or a colleague, and they wouldn't know I'm in a mad panic. My face will be just like it normally is, and I'll look normal, but internally, my heart's racing.'

Tina, a marketing manager, described her experience in terms of pins and needles: 'I have the strangest manifestations of my anxiety; I will get pins and needles in my hands. It manifests into a physical feeling which is awful.'

My own intense imposter feelings have triggered crippling stomach aches since my teenage years. Only now do I realise that my thinking caused these stomach aches. They came from the anxiety of wanting to get things 'right', worrying about not being 'good enough' and fearing I would be 'found out'. However, it wasn't until I started to research and understand the imposter phenomenon that I came to know that they were induced by my imposter-style thinking. Only then did they begin to diminish. When I mention these physical symptoms in workshops, there is often a ripple of recognition around the room, coupled with a sense of relief. Imposter feelings and their intensity may be felt by many, but they are not often spoken about. While my physical symptoms were in my stomach, others describe theirs as a tightness in the throat, nausea or even pins and needles, like Tina.

In summary, the experience of the imposter phenomenon varies from person to person, as does the frequency and intensity of imposter feelings. The experience is also not consistent within the same person and varies from situation to situation.[5] Mild, infrequent or one-off imposter experiences are not really an issue and may be associated with normal self-doubt. It is the intense, frequent imposter experiences that cause more problems and increase stress levels.

Imposter statements

How many of the statements below do you find yourself thinking or even saying aloud?

- Logically, I know that failure isn't fatal, but it sometimes feels like things will collapse if I don't do things right all of the time.
- If I make a mistake, it will prove I'm not up to the job.
- I can't let something go until it is perfect.
- Positive feedback makes me feel uncomfortable.
- If I am recommended for an award or promotion, I often think I don't deserve it.
- When I am successful at something, I worry about whether I can achieve the same standard again.

➤

- If I do something well, I am sure others would have been able to do the same.
- I often put my successes down to luck or hard work.

Note: this list is not a diagnosis or a validated questionnaire.

Reviewing this list and reflecting on how often you think like this can indicate the frequency or intensity of your imposter feelings.

Time in

- How frequent and intense are your imposter experiences?
- What physical symptoms, if any, do you have?
- In what way might you be holding yourself back?
- In what way do you compare yourself to others?

chapter 4

What's the problem?

'What is this self inside us,
this silent observer,
Severe and speechless critic,
who can terrorize us.'
T. S. Eliot, *The Elder Statesman*

Although the imposter phenomenon is usually discussed negatively, some people see their imposter feelings as akin to a superpower. They see it as something that motivates them to work harder and pushes them to achieve more. While this perspective may work well for some people, for others their imposter feelings may generate motivation at the expense of high levels of anxiety. This can lead to overwork and burnout, which is just the tip of the iceberg of the issues that experiencing the imposter phenomenon may cause.

One example of the negative impact of being motivated by imposter feelings was illustrated during a conversation at the end of one of my workshops. Two people stayed behind and described to me the sense of relief that they enjoy when they come to the end of the working day and they haven't been found out. But they went on to say that their anxiety levels were high again the next morning. At that point, their mind goes into overdrive, worrying about work, whether they are up to the task and what mistakes they might make. This cycle impacts their home lives, with their spouses commenting on their stress levels. So, although these two people felt their imposter feelings motivated them and helped them to work to a high standard, it was obviously at the expense of elevated stress levels and a negative impact on family life.

Similarly, Quinn, who works in human resources, set out what he saw as a benefit from his imposter-style anxiety and self-criticism. He felt that his reflection and self-criticism made him good at his job: 'So I can play those thoughts back afterwards, and it feeds into next time. I think that probably affects your feeling of imposter syndrome because you're constantly analysing and being self-critical. But it means you can be very good at what you do.'

But do you really want to be motivated by stress and anxiety to achieve a task or to reach a goal? Would it not be kinder to yourself to remove, or at least reduce, the stress levels and keep the motivation? What might it be like to maintain the quality of work and the satisfaction of reaching the goal but stop feeling like a fraud?

Lack of 'employee voice'

Imagine a workplace where nobody presents their ideas in meetings, decisions go unchallenged, and groupthink is the norm. Would that be a good place to work? Most people would say it's not an environment that they would choose. However, the anxiety associated with feeling like an imposter can prevent people from applying for or accepting a promotion,[1] inhibit them from speaking up in meetings and putting their ideas forward,[2] prevent them from asking questions or challenging decisions and increase their perfectionistic tendencies.[3] So they inadvertently create such a workplace.

Interestingly, some of these behaviours can be interpreted by an observer as shyness. Or it may be assumed that the individual doesn't know what to say or is disengaged from the topic. But that is generally not the case when someone is inhibited by their imposter feelings. The lack of 'voice' may be because they feel that they don't belong in the meeting, they think that they don't know enough about the subject, or perhaps believe that their opinion doesn't matter or won't be valued if it is voiced. It is probably not because they are shy, or because they don't know what to say, or because they are uninterested or disengaged. Their internal thought processes are more likely to be along the lines of: 'If I ask a question, they'll realise what I don't know,' 'They'll think I'm stupid raising this point,' or 'I should already know the answer to this, so I won't let on that I don't.'

Sometimes the hierarchy in organisations or meetings inhibits the inclination to speak up. In this case, the inner thinking might be: 'It's not my place to challenge,' 'I'm not senior enough,' 'Who am I to put forward a suggestion,' 'They won't listen to me,' 'I'm only a grade . . . ' or even 'I don't have enough experience to contribute to this meeting.'

These internal thoughts can also alter how questions are asked. Questions may be phrased in a way that diminishes the expertise of the questioner. Two of my research participants, Ellie and Ben, told me during their interviews that they caveat their statements with comments such as: 'This is a stupid question but . . . ' or 'This is probably really naive of me but . . . ' However, caveating questions or comments can make the individual appear to lack the relevant knowledge or come across as hesitant and under-confident. Whereas it is really the imposter feelings that make them reluctant to put their knowledge and expertise forward.

Imposter feelings can also surface after meetings, such as: 'Why was I invited?', 'Have I taken away the right points to pass back to my team?', 'Did I say the right thing?', 'I should have said more/less,' 'I should have said it differently.' All of these thoughts can create a spiral of negative self-talk, feeding the inner imposter feelings.

In a conversation I had with a workshop participant who was probably in his early thirties, I'll call him John, he told me he had recently been promoted to a leadership position. He described his imposter feelings and the stress he felt about the responsibility of attending meetings and accurately relaying the information back to his team. John wanted to ensure that he did it well, that he picked up all the right points and that the information he passed on was accurate – all laudable aims. But the stress his thinking was creating had started to take its toll on his well-being. The meetings were held with senior people at a high level in his organisation, and John didn't think he was the right person to attend them. It was his boss who had said he had to go. He was there because of his boss's positive opinion of him and his capabilities, which differed from his own negative self-perception. John was also invited to those meetings because of his position as a team leader. So he was the one who was able to relay the information back to the team, even though he didn't feel worthy of this responsibility.

It is hard to know how accurate John needed to be in his reporting back or how much detail he needed to go into. But to reduce the stress, we discussed reframing his imposter thoughts to ease the self-imposed pressure to be perfect. As he attends the meetings, he is the one with the information. So what he can do is 'the best of his ability with the knowledge and time he has available'. With that suggested reframe, John said he felt the pressure lift. He no longer had to relay what was said in the meeting word-for-word, or pass on all the information. He gave himself permission to pick out what he saw to be the key points and relay those to his team.

As you are the one who spends time in your own head, you are the one who can choose what to listen to. I'm not suggesting that controlling those imposter thoughts is easy; it takes time and effort. But it can be done. The first step is to recognise them. Then you can do something about the inner conversations.

Time in

Start to notice your inner thoughts . . .

- What internal comments have you made to yourself that hold you back from speaking up in certain situations?
  - Where do you think those thoughts come from?
  - What other childhood messages may be holding you back?
- How do you feel in meetings?
  - What encourages you to speak up?
  - What stops you?

Can it be a good thing?

British entrepreneur, podcaster and *Dragons' Den* investor Steven Bartlett posted a video on LinkedIn[4] talking about the benefits of 'imposter syndrome'. Bartlett suggested reframing feeling like an imposter as 'growth moments' and encouraged everyone to embrace their 'imposter'. However, the 'growth moments' Bartlett was referring to are stretches of your comfort zone and doing something you have not done before. As we have seen in Chapter 1, what you feel when doing something new and outside your comfort zone is normal self-doubt, not true imposter feelings. It is perfectly natural to feel out of your depth in a new situation.

What Bartlett is really talking about here is building confidence, and he has some good advice, but this is *not* the same as embracing the 'imposter syndrome'. This video is just one of the many frustrating examples on social media that confuse normal self-doubt with imposter feelings. The message that the imposter 'syndrome' is a good thing and should be embraced does not recognise the frequency, intensity or longevity of imposter feelings that some people experience throughout their career or even lifetime.

In academic circles a few articles argue positively for imposter feelings, suggesting that the imposter phenomenon has an upside. These articles typically highlight the benefits of imposter feelings in driving people to work extra hard to assuage feeling like an imposter.[5] In one example, Emily Hill interviewed 11 new administrative and professional employees at the University of Central Florida. Participants reported being driven to work extra hard, needing to prove themselves worthy and wanting to learn more to better themselves. However, as the participants were new in their roles, it isn't easy to assess whether they were experiencing normal self-doubt or true imposter feelings. Hill also interprets working extra hard as a positive aspect of feeling like an imposter. While this might be seen as a benefit to an organisation, it may not be beneficial for the individual. Working extra hard can be detrimental to well-being and lead to maladaptive perfectionism, where you set yourself exceedingly high standards and, consequently, burn out.[6] Those high standards may also have repercussions on your team. Your high standards towards yourself may make your team think they have to achieve the same, even if you do not expect them to.

In another academic article, Basima Tewfik, from Massachusetts Institute of Technology, discusses the positive benefits of feeling like an imposter. Tewfik suggests that people experiencing what she terms 'workplace imposter thoughts' are perceived by colleagues as more interpersonally effective and more 'other-focussed', making them more social and more likeable.[7] Tewfik suggests a positive relationship between workplace imposter thoughts and perceived interpersonal effectiveness. One of my participants, Nina, concurred with Tewfik's research. Nina suggested that imposter feelings 'prick your empathy a little. Because sometimes you see people acting in some way and, before you're too harsh, you stop and say: "Well, yeah, maybe they're feeling like this, or maybe they're feeling like I was feeling," and it softens your opinions a little bit'. However, it is unclear from Tewfik's research whether the interpersonal effectiveness identified would exist for everyone, including those who do not experience workplace imposter thoughts, or whether interpersonal effectiveness was something only those experiencing imposter thoughts expressed.

So one aspect to weigh up is whether the apparent benefits of experiencing the imposter phenomenon outweigh the downsides. Is working extra hard, being more effective in interpersonal relationships or being more empathic really a benefit of your imposter thoughts? Personally, I would rather forgo my imposter thoughts, reduce my stress levels and take a risk that my empathy and focus on other people will remain.

But it helps me stay humble

Another argument I frequently hear is that imposter feelings help people stay humble. But will you really lose your sense of humility if you stop feeling like an imposter? Will the opposite of experiencing the imposter phenomenon manifest as arrogance if you accept how good you really are?

Many people who report experiencing the imposter phenomenon seem to fear that accepting how good they are or owning their strengths will turn them into arrogant human beings. I genuinely don't think that would be the case. However, some people strongly equate their imposter feelings with humility. For example, Quinn has been keen to avoid becoming arrogant and reflected on the impact on his confidence over the years: 'If I'm confident about something, I want it to be genuine. I'm very self-critical and it probably hasn't done my confidence any good over the years. I've never wanted to be overconfident.'

When you meet someone who knows what they can do and who also acknowledges what they can't do, you don't automatically assume they are over-confident or arrogant. Unless they tell you they are arrogant, as one well-known Cambridge entrepreneur said to me over dinner at King's College several years ago: 'You don't get to be where I am without being arrogant,' he claimed. Arrogance is putting yourself above others and believing you are superior. Whereas someone who knows what they can do and what they can't, without diminishing themselves, has a healthy sense of self and their capabilities.

Researchers at Flinders University in Adelaide, Australia,[8] defined workplace and leader arrogance as 'a misplaced sense of superiority, manifested as disparaging behaviour towards others'. Reducing or removing your imposter feelings, accepting the positive view that others have of you and internalising positive feedback will not automatically give you a misplaced sense of superiority. Nor will it encourage you to behave disparagingly towards others. But it will reduce the stress and anxiety associated with imposter feelings. So rather than trying to stay humble, perhaps we could all embody the view of C. S. Lewis, who purportedly said:

'True humility is not thinking less of yourself, but thinking of yourself less.'

Accepting positive comments from others won't make you arrogant. Dismissing them doesn't make you humble.

Is it stressful? You bet!

For some people, their imposter feelings fall into what Pauline Clance described as 'few' or 'moderate' imposter experiences[9] (mild or medium cheese). For others, they fall into the category of 'frequent' or 'intense' (extra-strong cheese). For people with few or moderate imposter feelings, the stress levels will be lower than for those with frequent or intense imposter feelings, for whom the experience of imposter thoughts can be very stressful. The indication from research is that frequent or intense imposter feelings increase anxiety and reduce the sense of well-being[10] and happiness.[11]

In an online study of 190 individuals in leadership positions, researchers at Goethe University in Frankfurt[12] looked at anxiety resulting from imposter feelings. They found that imposter anxiety is more likely to be cognitive anxiety rather than emotional anxiety, i.e. thinking rather than feeling. This indicates that imposter thoughts are more likely to be linked to self-doubt, worry or low confidence rather than the emotive extremes associated with clinical anxiety. But that may not be the case for everyone. In this extract from Mark, a broker in his fifties, he describes the impact his anxiety had and how he struggled to find the courage to carry on at work due to a lack of support: 'In the last [work]place, unfortunately, I concluded I couldn't find enough of it [courage] because there wasn't enough support around me. That led me to very high stress levels. It was so awful; there were occasions when my head was just spinning and I was going, "come on, you can do this, you can do this," and then I'd go, "no, I can't" – and I'd go and lie on the bed and cry.' Thankfully, Mark left that organisation and moved to one where he found a more supportive workplace culture and a more supportive manager.

As well as the stress and anxiety caused by imposter feelings, feeling like an imposter can also impact our behaviour. Research indicates this may lead to procrastination and perfectionism and impact how we view failure, which I will cover next.

Procrastination, perfectionism and failure

As mentioned in Chapter 2, self-handicapping is the creation of an impediment to your performance to provide an excuse for potential failure.[13] Procrastination and perfectionism are examples of self-handicapping behaviours. A fear of failure is also associated with the imposter phenomenon.

Procrastination

Procrastination is one of the behaviours that can result from feeling like an imposter in the workplace. Psychologist Dr Thomas Curran describes it as not a time management problem but an anxiety management problem.[14] Procrastination may result in tasks being completed in a last-minute rush, so the end result is not up to the standard that you would like it to be. Or you might miss a deadline altogether so that you can take the time you need to complete the task to your own high standards.[15] However, your manager and colleagues are unlikely to be aware of your inner thought processes (none of us is a mind reader). They will see a behaviour of delaying starting tasks or failing to complete them on time and may misinterpret this as laziness, lack of interest or lack of ability. I have spoken to many managers who, on reflection, realise that they have lost some good team members through misinterpreting behaviour that was probably caused by imposter feelings, which they did not know about and had not considered.

Perfectionism

Perfectionism can be driven by the fear of failure, not being good enough and a desire to avoid mistakes, and is associated with imposter feelings.[16] Research with college students in America also found that feelings of shame were associated with making mistakes and increased imposter feelings.[17]

Those who experience frequent and intense imposter feelings have high expectations of themselves, such as Ben, who realises: 'I shouldn't be expecting myself to know every little thing. And trying to remind myself that, if I can do 78 per cent of my daily tasks, that's more than enough. That's more than they [the employer] expect from me.'

I have had my own issues with perfectionism since childhood (and still do to some extent). I have an early memory from when

I was about six years old. I was sitting with my mum on an old wooden chest by an upstairs window in our house, overlooking the Lincolnshire marshes near the seaside resort of Skegness. Having just washed my hair, my mum was telling me a little ditty as she combed through the curls and tangles: 'There was a little girl who had a little curl right in the middle of her forehead. When she was good, she was very, very good. But when she was bad, she was horrid.' Now I'm sure it was meant as a simple rhyme, but I thought it meant I had to be good because I certainly didn't want to be horrid. That, to me, meant being perfect.

It wasn't until I was in my forties, when I learnt about the imposter phenomenon and the links with perfectionism, that I started to make fundamental changes to my perfectionistic tendencies. Before then, if you were to cut me in half, you would have found the words 'must be perfect' running through my core, like a stick of Skegness rock. Even though I knew, logically, that we learn from making mistakes, in my mind mistakes were to be avoided at all costs, and I still have to catch myself when I start thinking like this. I now realise that I am not alone in this way of thinking. Many people who experience the imposter phenomenon have perfectionistic tendencies, which can create a mindset that anything less than perfect is not good enough.[18]

Another issue with perfectionism is that the fear of not doing something perfectly can prevent you from even trying.[19] Perhaps you stop doing something you enjoy, such as a sport or playing a musical instrument, because you can't do it well enough (according to your own high standards). Or maybe you are like Cleo, who takes a compliment on one of her skills as criticism about another: 'I do get comments thrown at me, well not thrown at, but comments that are actually quite complimentary, but I take it in a negative light. If it's a compliment on my artistic skills, is that also a criticism that I'm not good enough at work?'

It is easy to internalise the idea that you should get everything right all of the time, that you should be perfect. Of course, that is unrealistic. We are human beings and we are 'perfectly imperfect' (to paraphrase American professor, researcher and author Brené

Brown.)[20] Unrealistic expectations and exceptionally high standards fuel imposter feelings.[21] If we don't achieve the level of success we expect or we fail to live up to our own standards, our own thinking can come down on us like a ton of bricks.

Many people consider perfectionism – completing work to a high standard – a laudable trait. Yet sometimes it can be helpful to ditch perfectionistic tendencies and adopt a more pragmatic approach. One that aims for 'good enough' rather than perfection. This might be helpful when there is a looming deadline, when there are other pressing work tasks to be completed, or when you are overworking a task and not making beneficial amendments. Some people may also have perfectionistic standards for competitive reasons, i.e. to *be* the best.

An example of someone towards the opposite end of the perfectionistic scale is my husband, who built a successful career working in high-tech product development by taking a pragmatic approach. This is an industry where technology moves fast and new products need to be brought to market in a timely manner. Thinking about what the product needs, doing that and nothing more is important. As a result, he learned to take a pragmatic, 'good enough' approach. This now serves him well in his second career as a teacher, where trying to do everything perfectly would be a surefire path to burnout. It is an approach I am still learning and my perfectionist tendencies sometimes frustrate him!

Perfectionistic tendencies are not all bad or negative. Psychologists differentiate between maladaptive (negative) perfectionism and adaptive (positive) perfectionism.[22] Maladaptive perfectionism can induce over-work and high stress levels, potentially leading to burnout, while adaptive perfectionism ensures that standards are met.

Failure

Fear of failure is something individuals experiencing imposter thoughts live with on a regular basis. It can be a fear of being incompetent, making a mistake, failing to live up to expectations, or not being good enough. This is often a low-level fear for many people experiencing imposter thoughts. Fay, the chief risk officer we met earlier, described the impact of this low-level fear as 'death by a thousand paper cuts':

'It fades and it amplifies depending on the circumstances, but for me it is always present. It is just how big or small it is. If it's loud, it means that I am much more likely to deal with it. When it's quiet, it is death by a thousand paper cuts. It's then that I haven't realised, and I quite often won't realise, how difficult I'm actually finding things. And that's when it grows because it really does cut away at my confidence.'

Another of my participants, Ellie, head of risk at an insurance firm, told me about the first time she failed an exam. She explained that the online teaching format was not conducive to her learning style, thereby finding an external reason for the failure. While this may be an accurate reason, it may have been mentioned because Ellie felt she needed to present an excuse for failing. Finding an external cause for failure can be easier than reflecting on the possible internal reasons, such as the fact that we did not meet the required standard or did not put in the necessary work. Imposter-style thinking usually internalises failure and externalises success, but this example from Ellie shows that there is no one-size-fits-all list of behaviours.

At times imposter-style thinking can also prevent people from even trying. Whether that is sitting an exam, applying for a job or promotion, or putting your idea forward in a meeting. The fear of failure or rejection can be so intense that it is avoided at all costs. In Chapter 7 we will look at how to overcome that fear. Of course, no one likes to fail. But an intense fear of failure is one part of imposter-style thinking.[23] You can have a fear or dislike of failure without feeling like an imposter.

Time in

- -

- Are your imposter feelings a good thing for you?
- What stresses, if any, do they cause?
- When might you procrastinate?
- What reaction have you had to the idea of letting go of perfectionism?

- -

chapter 5

Why it matters at work

'When you plant lettuce, if it does not grow well you don't blame the lettuce. You look for reasons it is not doing well. It may need fertilizer, or more water, or less sun. You never blame the lettuce.'

Thich Nhat Hanh, *At Home in the World*

While imposter thoughts and feelings affect the individual, the impact can be much broader. As mentioned in Chapter 2, organisational culture and the environment can lead to employees developing imposter feelings. For example, walking onto an esteemed research campus, working in a prestigious building or with distinguished colleagues can trigger imposter thoughts. This chapter explores the potential impact of the imposter phenomenon on productivity, teams and organisations, an area that has so far received very little research. What leaders and managers can do to provide support to others and mitigate the impact of imposter thoughts is covered in Chapter 9.

Productivity and perfectionism

As an employer or manager, you may initially see the imposter phenomenon as a positive due to the extra effort and productivity from the people who experience it.[1] In the long term, this extra effort is unlikely to be positive for the individual and may also have consequences for the team. Dealing with imposter feelings through overworking and perfectionism is very tiring. Work often spills over into evenings and weekends. This can harm mental health and well-being, potentially leading to reduced productivity over the long term and even absences and sickness.

Additionally, imposter feelings do not always translate into increased productivity, even though longer hours may be being worked. As mentioned in the previous chapter, procrastination is linked to imposter feelings. Just stop for a moment to consider the impact on productivity levels and on the wider team if time is being frittered away, finding non-essential activities to keep 'busy' at work and not tackle the task at hand. As procrastination increases, productivity levels fall. (I am reflecting on this last sentence as I write it – there are many small jobs that start to look very appealing when there is a book to write!)

Managers and team leaders could look for a reduction in productivity levels as an indication of imposter feelings among team members. If someone is not as productive as they used to be, are they procrastinating? If they are procrastinating, why? Look for reasons rather than judging them as lazy, disengaged or uncaring about their work.

Perfectionism is another time stealer with a potentially negative impact on productivity. People have told me that they can spend a day preparing for a one-hour meeting to ensure they are able to answer every question that might possibly crop up. Surely that cannot be a good use of time. Another way perfectionism may manifest is when producing spreadsheets or writing reports. Colour-coding the spreadsheet columns so the colours match and look pretty is another example of perfectionism I have heard from many people. In reality, it is the spreadsheet's content that really matters, not the colours (except for legibility). Double-checking every full stop, every comma and every title alignment in reports, as well as reading and rereading your work to iron out any possible errors, also takes an enormous amount of time. As we all know, spotting mistakes when reading your own work isn't easy, so the time is not necessarily being well spent.

For some reports the fine details are important, depending on the purpose and the reader. Getting a second or third pair of eyes to review your work can be helpful. In those cases, calling the work a draft can encourage people with imposter feelings to let go of 'unperfected' work and reduce that inner 'ouch' when someone makes a suggestion to improve it.

Generally speaking, it is the content people are interested in, not the font, formatting or colour coordination. To prevent repeated tweaking of your work, who can you ask to review it and to spot what amendments are really necessary? What are the likely consequences if it is not perfect? Two friends proofread my PhD thesis, my three supervisors read it, and I read it and reread it more times than I dare to count – yet, there was still a typo, a couple of grammatical errors and a spelling mistake that one of my examiners picked up. But that didn't mean I failed my PhD; it just meant I needed to make a few changes before the final submission. My perfectionist imposter feelings reared up at that point, and I had to try really hard to allow myself to be ok about the changes . . . after all, nothing and no one is perfect, not even you or me.

Time in

- Are your imposter feelings causing you to procrastinate or work to a higher standard than is necessary?

- Where does the standard really lie?

- How can you assess whether you are meeting that standard? Enlist others to help you.

- How can you begin to tackle the main task? One small piece at a time?

- Try sending out a draft of your work for someone else to review. They can then guide you on what else needs to be done – which may not be as much as you think.

Delegation and potential bias

If you are leading a team and you, as the team leader or manager, experience imposter thoughts, then some research suggests you might be biased in how you delegate work. Researcher Myriam Bechtoldt,[2] at the Frankfurt School of Finance & Management, presented hypothetical task-based scenarios to 190 managers and asked them to select which of four employee profiles they would delegate the work to. There were six tasks: three were described as routine, and three were described as challenging. Two of the four hypothetical employees were said to be self-confident in their abilities, and the other two were described as secretly doubting their abilities. All four were described as being conscientious and motivated.

The study found that managers who experienced imposter feelings preferred to delegate both the routine and the challenging tasks to the self-doubting employees, not to the confident employees, as we might expect. There may be a number of reasons for this, but these are not clear from the research. Perhaps managers who experience imposter feelings do not want to be challenged. Possibly self-doubting employees are seen as more submissive and less likely to challenge their manager than confident employees. Perhaps there is a bias towards delegating to people who are also self-doubting, maybe because the self-doubting manager feels more empathetic towards them.

Whatever the reason, there could be unexpected consequences from this biased delegation. While Bechtoldt's study used hypothetical scenarios, in the actual workplace delegating more tasks to employees who are high in self-doubt could put them under increased pressure, potentially overloading them with work. Given their self-doubt, these individuals may be less likely to ask for help or admit that they are not coping. This may increase levels of anxiety, overwork and the potential for burnout.

Loss of talent and over-reward

Another issue arising from the imposter phenomenon at work is a loss of talent. This can have both a personal and an organisational impact. Research indicates[3] that those experiencing the imposter phenomenon may not apply for promotions, even when they are ready or when their manager suggests that they do so. At other times, it may be that people do not realise their own knowledge, skills or capabilities, so they underplay their talent. Or talent goes unrecognised by managers or organisations. Sometimes it could even mean people leaving jobs that they are very capable of doing if, on the inside, they feel that they are not good enough, leading them to choose to move to a less demanding role.

Over the years, several people have told me that they opted to demote themselves and move to a less stressful job because they didn't feel they deserved the more senior role. However, the stress didn't seem to come so much from the job as from thinking of themselves as unworthy of their higher position.

My research participants cited several examples of imposter feelings holding back their careers. In Ellie's case, she had been headhunted recently by an agency for a senior role. Yet, instead of applying for the role herself, she tipped off a colleague and suggested that he apply instead because Ellie thought the role was too senior for her. As she was telling her colleague about the role, she started to think: 'Why am I doing this? If you were of a different mindset, you would just wing it.' Then, when Ellie was offered a promotion at work, she very nearly turned it down. Instead, she assuaged her imposter feelings by asking for the job title to be changed from director to head of department because she felt she did not warrant the title of director. When Ellie spoke to me, she was still dismissing the revised title, saying: 'Even that's a bit of a nonsense because you know I'm not head of department. I'm just part of the team. I'm not the head of it. I'm head of a part of it.'

Another of my participants, Una, recalled the daily stresses she experienced when she was in charge of a project: 'I was all right with my little lane, but I was suddenly directing the project and asking them questions and trying to get their buy-in and their agreement to stuff. There were people from IT who had been there for 30 years and probably spent most of their 30 years doing the work, and me . . . I was literally waiting for somebody to say, "who are you to ask me that?", "who are you to tell me this is what I need to do?". Even sending communications out to people, I was sending them thinking, "there's going to be something wrong; somebody is going to come back to me and tell me that I've dropped a massive ball!".'

When this is the daily thinking, it is easy to understand why people opt to demote themselves to be relieved of the stress. But the fact is, these people are doing a good job. They are qualified and capable. The organisation loses out because their employees' talent is not being used to its full extent.

The individual loses out too, as a result of their own actions. There is a concept psychologists call 'perceived over-reward', which occurs in situations where the recipient considers the responsibilities involved in a promotion or job offer to be over and above their capabilities and can be a cause for imposter feelings.[4] In these circumstances, they turn the job down or move roles to correct the perceived over-reward. Another example of perceived over-reward is where feedback, or an appraisal, is seen to be too glowing. So, the feedback or the appraisal results are ignored, dismissed or excused.

Psychologists have linked the response to a perceived over-reward by individuals experiencing imposter feelings to the concept of 'equity'. Equity theory suggests that the individual will take steps to correct any perceived under-reward or over-reward.[5] This means they are likely to downplay any successes or, as mentioned earlier, turn down promotions.[6] While that might alleviate the imposter feelings, it does so by removing the stressor, not by eliminating the imposter feelings themselves. So at an individual level, imposter feelings can be an inner barrier to career development. But if you can get your imposter thoughts in check, with support from your manager and the organisation, there is no need for self-initiated demotion, self-deprecation or self-imposed career stagnation.

In the following examples, Roger and Tina share their internal conversations about a time when they were offered a promotion or when deciding to apply for a new job.

Roger, a marketing and communications manager in his mid-forties, was encouraged to apply for the role of head of IT. He described the benefit of doing so as well as how it triggered his imposter feelings: 'I had quite a few people going, "Oh, you should go for that." So I went for it, but I'll be honest, all the way through I was thinking, "I have no idea what I'm doing." But going for that interview helped me because it crystallised some of the stuff that I've done and helped me think, "No, I did do that." But it also amplified the whole, "oh, my god, they're gonna find out that I've actually no idea about IT at all".'

Tina is now a successful marketing manager but, when she recalled applying for the role, she said: 'I just couldn't write my CV;

I couldn't bring myself do it because I was thinking "what if I write it and it turns out I haven't done anything for three years" – even though I clearly have!'

As Roger's and Tina's examples show, creating a CV or going for an interview, while stressful, can help crystalise your achievements in your own eyes. It can also help you to think objectively about your knowledge, skills and abilities.

Time in

- Have your imposter feelings held you back in your career? What action did you take?
- Have you had an interview recently where you reviewed your skill set?
- When did you last update your CV?
- How objective were you when writing about yourself?
- Who can you ask to help write or review your CV?

So how do people manage to have successful careers, despite their inner imposter feelings? This is something I have reflected on over the years. In my case, I look back at the organisational culture at Barclays Bank when I worked there in the 1980s and 1990s. At the time, the process of promoting staff was simply to tell people where they would be working next, in what role and at what grade, much like a posting in the military. Sometimes, the changes were made at short notice. In some cases, you could be told on a Friday morning where you would be working the following Monday, or you might get a week's notice. I don't recall any discussions with my managers about the promotions or changes in roles. It was a given that you would accept them. Later, the bank started advertising jobs internally and inviting people to apply. While I'm not recommending military-style postings, I do wonder whether my career would have been so successful if I had had to apply for every job and every promotion rather than being promoted without my input or initiative.

Meetings – stress, silence and safety

Imposter feelings also affect how likely people are to speak up at work. Does the organisation or team you work in have an open culture? Is it one where people feel safe to challenge ideas, to voice their own suggestions, to be creative and develop new ways of working? Do you have a manager who listens to their team members? Do you work in an organisation that values ideas and suggestions from its employees? Are you encouraged to speak up and challenge the existing ways of working to develop something better? This type of workplace is, for some people, a pipe dream.

As mentioned in Chapter 4, 'employee voice' is a term sometimes used to describe using your voice at work to constructively challenge the status quo, with the aim of changing things for the better.[7] Or in academic-speak, an 'upward-directed, discretionary verbal behaviour with the intent to benefit the organisation'.[8] An important factor must be in place for employees to feel able to use their voice: psychological safety.[9] A psychologically safe environment is one where people are comfortable expressing their thoughts and ideas without fear of embarrassment, ridicule or worse. By encouraging a culture of 'transparency, curiosity and growth', research suggests that psychological safety can help individuals to overcome the 'self-critical and fixed mindsets associated with imposter feelings'.[10]

Sadly, describing a safe and supportive environment and its benefits is easier than creating it or finding it in the workplace. Most of the participants in my study expressed a reluctance to speak up in meetings and held themselves back from asking questions or presenting ideas. This means organisations are losing out on potentially valuable contributions. They are at risk of groupthink, and managers and team leaders may believe they have assent through silence rather than seeking active verbal agreement.

Meetings are an everyday occurrence and a necessary part of workplace communications. But have you ever considered how stressful they can be for some people? I certainly hadn't before undertaking my research. Nearly every participant I spoke to mentioned meetings as an exacerbating factor for their imposter feelings. The most stressful meetings were not, as you might think, the big, important presentations. A lot of the stress was caused by weekly team briefings, project updates and regular one-to-one meetings with line managers.

Meetings can generate anxiety about what other people think. If you speak up, will other people think you are stupid for asking that question or making that suggestion? One-to-one meetings with managers can increase the fear that 'this will be the time that they will find me out'. Meetings can also increase imposter thoughts of not being good enough in the role because you 'should' already know the details of what is being discussed.

Ellie, one of my participants, was concerned that if she asked for clarification on what was being discussed or what a particular acronym meant, others would look at her as if she had 'fallen out of a tree'. This reluctance to ask for clarification was also mentioned by Una, who, in her role as a team manager, said that she has been 'on calls where others have used a terminology all the way through, and I've not had a scooby [clue] what they're talking about'.

In addition to inhibiting contributions to discussions, imposter feelings also create a reluctance to ask questions or challenge decisions. Lisa, associate director for a financial company, comments: 'I wouldn't want to say anything in case, in case I looked like I didn't know what I was talking about!' Managing the perceptions of others was also important to Pat, who was in her fifties and head of HR at an insurance firm. Her concern was 'worrying what other people's perception will be of me if I ask something. "What's she asked that for? Why doesn't she know that?" So, it's about managing other people's perceptions, being concerned about other people's perceptions of me.'

This reluctance to contribute to meetings focuses on a fear that others will perceive you negatively. This fear is exacerbated if you feel that you are not worthy of the job you are doing and that you might be 'found out'.

So should you be so concerned about what others think? To paraphrase the well-known quote:

'What other people think of you is none of your business.'

Yet, there is a world of difference between using this quote as your mantra and actually overcoming the fear of being judged negatively.

How many times have you acted like Pat, head of HR, who says that she still doesn't like to ask questions in meetings yet regrets hesitating when others often get in first: 'I mean, this happened yesterday, there was a big group session, and there was a Q&A section at the end. And there were about three questions that were asked where I thought, "I wanted to ask that question" and I thought, "why didn't I ask those questions?"' Or are you more like Kelly, head of client services, who says: 'They must know what I'm thinking because it's really obvious; they must all know it, they're just skirting around it. And then, eventually, I realise in these meetings that I do know what I'm doing, and I should speak up and say it. It is not known by everybody.'

Interestingly, there was no consensus in my research on whether online meetings were better or worse than in-person meetings when it came to triggering imposter feelings. It was very much down to individual preferences. For some participants, online meetings were preferable to in-person because they could, in Cleo's words, fact-check behind the scenes or text a colleague for support: 'Very often, it [imposter] happens more in meetings, where you're in a live situation session and you can't fact-check your belief thoroughly before you make an intervention.' Ellie also preferred online meetings as she could attend without having to look at the 50-plus other people in the meeting, something that helped her focus and stay in the present. Quinn, in his role as HR manager, admits to not always speaking up in online meetings: 'Sometimes, we have big team meetings, and I find it uncomfortable. You know, when you've got up to 80 people in a Zoom room, and you're having discussions. I let someone else do the talking.' Quinn also gave an example of someone else's behaviour in a meeting that would trigger his imposter thoughts: 'I suppose if sometimes there's a meeting where people are very aggressive and bullish, usually it's men, but not necessarily, that's one where I'm less comfortable of being assertive. I'm not one of these table-thumping types'.

For other participants, in-person meetings were better as they could gauge the likely reactions in the room more easily before speaking up. The meeting environment, whether online or in-person, can also be exhausting and induce physical sensations of anxiety. Roger, in his forties, a marketing and communications manager with an insurance firm, said: 'It's not the actual work. It's just that functioning and trying to present yourself in such a way that people take you as credible . . . it's a big emotional and mental effort to do that. The more involved I am in the meeting and the more central I am to the meeting, the more I fret. So it's just trying to cope, to get through without feeling physically sick.'

For some people, meetings are so stressful that simply attending them requires a lot of courage. Lisa, associate director at a finance company, described a courageous act as 'just getting into a meeting to start off with, without crying the night before'.

An ingenious way of getting views heard in meetings had been developed by both Quinn and Simeon. They had both found a way to avoid speaking up in meetings by using their line managers to ask questions for them. They did this by feeding key points to their respective managers to raise in meetings, or they raised the points with their managers after the meeting:

> Quinn: 'Rather than comment at the meeting, I will comment after the meeting to my manager, just to get my point of view across and have a discussion with them. It's partly avoidance, but partly it's communicating via what is, to me, a safer means.'
>
> Simeon: 'Something that happens quite often, if I'm really not confident, is feeding my line manager all of the answers and coaching them to say what I'm not brave enough to say myself. So, effectively, they become the confident actor that you would like to be yourself.'

However, by using this strategy, neither Quinn nor Simeon are likely to be given credit for their ideas. That will probably go to their managers. But at least their ideas will be heard, even if the credit goes elsewhere.

Psychologists have termed behaviour that involves not revealing your true ideas or opinions 'intellectual inauthenticity'.[11] Choosing not to speak your authentic opinions, remaining silent or telling people what you think they want to hear avoids judgement from others. This avoidance, or inauthentic behaviour, helps to maintain imposter feelings.

Another behaviour that those experiencing high imposter feelings may display is to downplay their intelligence.[12] One way of doing this is to caveat suggestions or preface questions, to 'play it safe' rather than assert honest opinions. Cleo said she heavily caveats her suggestions and uses phrases such as 'from my knowledge' or 'from my understanding', 'I believe' or 'my understanding is this'. Roger also said he is very guarded in how he phrases his statements, using 'well, I might be wrong . . . but do this'. And Ellie said that she 'always badges it like: "This is a stupid question, but . . . " or "You know this is probably really naive of me, but . . . ".' Whereas Holly counters her own suggestions: 'When you do something, you almost immediately say: "I've done this, but it probably isn't very good." Or "I've done it, but I'm sure you can improve on it".'

Caveating suggestions also happens in online group chats, such as Slack channels. Ben chooses not to assert his knowledge just in case he isn't correct. Instead, he puts his ideas forward in a different way: 'In the chat, you can kinda say, "this is what it might be, but is anyone else available to confirm this?"'

Whether using caveats is a positive or negative coping strategy is a matter of opinion. Giving caveats may help you feel more comfortable offering your ideas. But beware, there is a risk that suggestions and ideas are offered in such a heavily caveated way that others may discount or overlook your contributions. This can lead to a lack of recognition of your knowledge, skills and experience, which may impact your performance reviews and promotional opportunities.

Nevertheless, some of the concerns about speaking up in meetings will be valid. Most of us like to be liked and want to be thought of positively by others. Speaking up in meetings can indeed carry a risk. Research by Ethan Burris[13] at the University of Texas found that managers perceived feedback differently when employees used their 'voice' in a supportive or in a challenging manner. In the research, managers said they wanted team members who would positively challenge decisions to aid decision making. However, employees in Burris's study who used a challenging 'voice' were given lower performance ratings. In contrast, employees who engaged more frequently in a supportive 'voice' received more favourable performance ratings. Interestingly, Burris's research found that experts using a challenging voice were received more favourably than non-experts using the same voice.

Maybe this is the incentive for those of us with imposter feelings to stop downplaying our expertise. If we use our knowledge and expertise and voice our ideas as an expert, we are more likely to be viewed in a favourable light.

Additional research by Detert and Burris[14] found that organisations and managers could reduce the intensity of employees' imposter feelings by providing support and listening to their concerns and ideas. Taking time to support and listen to staff also increased mental well-being and boosted contributions in meetings. The benefits may not only be in relieving the stress of imposter feelings for the individual but may also benefit the organisation as a whole.

Another issue stemming from people feeling like imposters at work is reduced creativity within a team or organisation. This can result from not speaking up in meetings, not challenging decisions or not putting forward ideas. Imposter thinking can encourage us to think that we should only put forward ideas that will be well received by others, otherwise we should stay silent. But creativity happens when ideas are discussed, shaped and developed. Ideas rarely come out fully formed in their first iteration. So, in the words of Charlie Mackesy, who encourages us to embrace creativity and imagination in his 2018 TEDx talk, we need to be willing to 'relish the mess'.[15]

Staying silent and not using our voice, whether supportive or challenging, may also encourage groupthink.[16] This can happen when a sense of belonging and conforming to the group becomes more important than critical thinking or evaluating alternative ideas. Reframing the mindset of how contributions can be received, promoting the benefit of discussions and debate and seeing this more positively might increase the likelihood of people with imposter feelings speaking up and, in doing so, avoiding groupthink.

Here's Cleo on her desire to ensure her contributions at work are correct: 'Outside of a live meeting environment, I think I have more confidence because I can triple-check, you know, quadruple-check what I'm about to submit. And know that front and back, upside down, everything is right to the best of my knowledge. In a live meeting situation, I hesitate to make interventions.' What Cleo is describing is the benefit feeling prepared makes to her confidence and her willingness, or not, to speak up in meetings. However, being prepared and over-preparing are two different things, as discussed in part two.

Time in

- How do you feel about voicing your ideas or concerns in meetings?
- Do you have a preference for online meetings or in-person meetings? Why do you think that is the case?
- How can you ensure your ideas are heard without using caveats or being submissive?
- Where do you have expertise that would benefit others?
- How will you share that expertise in the future?

part 2

———

Coping strategies to help overcome the imposter phenomenon

chapter 6

What do others do about it?

'Maybe I'm not as useless as I think; it's just this voice telling me that.

I am qualified to do my job.'

Kelly, *research participant*

There is currently very little research into how people cope with their imposter feelings at work or what can be done to lessen these feelings. Understanding coping strategies has been the main focus of my research. In this chapter you will hear more from my research participants and how they coped with their imposter feelings, together with findings from other recent studies. The chapter is structured around the four themes I identified in my research: external support, belonging and otherness, donning armour and finding courage.

Back in 2018, a TED video was recorded by Elizabeth Cox[1] in which she suggested strategies for coping with the imposter syndrome. In the video, Cox suggests that there are three things that can help reduce imposter thoughts. The first two are knowing that the imposter syndrome is a 'thing' and talking about it with others, both of which have been found to be very helpful. She also suggests collecting and documenting positive feedback, which, while helpful, is not enough to combat imposter feelings in and of itself. In Chapter 7, I explain why I think that is the case and how you can use positive feedback to help combat feelings of imposterism.

My participants often described their coping strategies as 'fighting' their imposter feelings, putting on 'armour' or going into 'battle'. It takes an enormous amount of mental energy and time to prepare for battle and go into the fight, as well as courage. Thankfully, my research found some strategies that do not require the same amount of time or mental energy, but they may require courage to implement.

Anecdotally, many people would not describe themselves as courageous, preferring to use words such as 'being brave' or 'having gumption'. But being brave, having gumption or being courageous certainly does not mean having to do things alone. One of my favourite quotes from Charlie Mackesy's delightful book *The Boy, the Mole, The Fox and The Horse*[2] is:

> '"What is the bravest thing you've ever said?", asked the boy.
>
> "Help", said the horse, "Asking for help isn't giving up. It's refusing to give up".'

You may need to reach out and ask for support; don't assume that support will automatically be given when it is needed. Not because people don't want to support you, but because they believe you don't need it – they see a capable, confident, competent you and may not realise what is happening on the inside. Help from others and external support was one of the main coping strategies identified in my research interviews.

External support

It is easier to diminish or even banish your imposter thoughts if you have support along the way. Support may come from any number of sources, including spouses, romantic partners, family, friends, managers, colleagues, mentors and role models.

In this example, Jean, head of marketing at an insurance firm, recalls the support she received from a male colleague in a difficult meeting:

> 'I can remember being in a meeting with about 10 other people. I was only about six months in and, at that point, I knew nothing about insurance. Back then I was still learning the jargon that's flying around, and the knowledge that some of these people have goes back years. It's all going over my head; I'm out of my depth, but I know that we need this e-trading solution but I can't back it up. I'm sitting there in this meeting, and even though I'm 42, I could feel tears coming, and I thought, "oh, my god, you cannot do this in front of these people." And I managed to choke it back. One of the guys in the room recognised that I was struggling. He could see I was struggling and without doing anything specific, he came in and supported the conversation. Afterwards, he came and found me and said "that was a really tough meeting. You did really well. There's history here you don't know; I can help you. Why don't we go and do lunch." And he took me away, but he didn't know how close I was [to crying]. I subsequently told him, "do you know, x years ago, that's where I was, this is what you did for me and it made a world of difference." And he was junior to me.'

This example illustrates the nuances that can be picked up in a face-to-face meeting by colleagues. It also illustrates how momentous a seemingly small touch can be, such as a supportive comment made in a meeting or lunch together after a difficult meeting, and the positive impact these small acts of kindness and support can have. In online meetings it is more difficult to see when someone else needs support (indeed, some people may turn their cameras off so you cannot see that they are struggling). It also requires more effort to offer the support once the meeting has ended. But that doesn't mean it can't be done.

Another of my participants, Nina, also spoke about the benefit of receiving support from colleagues, which she described as gentle nudges of encouragement: 'There was always someone that was a bit more encouraging. Maybe the one who was sitting next to you who would nudge you and say: "Maybe you should ask that".' These nudges can be made in face-to-face meetings, but I have also heard examples of nudges being given in online meetings through text messages or WhatsApp chats while the meeting is in progress.

Some of the most rewarding times in my professional life have been when I've provided that little bit of support or nudge to make a difference. I can recall facilitating an online workshop where all except one of the participants were female. I don't remember what I said to the one male participant as he joined the workshop but later, in a LinkedIn message, he reminded me that I referred to him as an ally. He said he is forever thankful, as my way of welcoming him helped him feel included and stopped him from feeling like an outsider.

External support can be a real benefit,[3] but not everyone has someone close to them who they can rely on. When support from others isn't there, or it isn't obvious, a (perceived) lack of support can increase imposter thoughts and feelings. Despite the stress and anxiety caused by a lack of support at work, a couple of my interviewees talked about having a 'have to' attitude. Amy spoke about finding the courage to carry on as something that is 'non-negotiable' and Ben described his approach to work as one where 'I can't just walk away. I can't not turn up on a Monday; I have to go in.'

If you find yourself in this position, where might you turn for support? Perhaps to friends or family members? Or daring to share your vulnerability with colleagues to garner their support?

Time in

- Have you recently made an effort to reach out to a colleague and ask how they are?
- When did someone reach out to support you?
- Have you recently asked for support from someone?
- How comfortable do you feel opening up to others about your imposter feelings?
- If you have received support from someone, have you been back to that person to thank them?

If you are managing other people, imagine the amount of stress you could relieve if a team member no longer thinks that they have to hide their imposter feelings. If they can tell you that they think they might not be up to the job, and you can show them the evidence that they are truly capable and doing their job to a good standard, the impact and relief could be massive. Ellie illustrated this when she talked about the impact her HR manager had made: 'She's absolutely got 100 per cent faith in me to do what I'm doing and that that has made a massive difference. She reassures me.' In the IT department where Ben works, a change of manager to someone more supportive had a hugely positive impact on him and the team: 'We've had a new manager within the last four months and she's been brilliant. She's got our backs; she says we've been doing so well. It's nice to have that kind of reassurance.'

Support from managers is not always obvious and is not always given directly. Iris, in her mid-thirties and working in learning and development, tells of the encouragement she took from a talk given by her CEO to the whole organisation where he shared his experiences of feeling like an imposter: 'I just remembered what our CEO had said, which I found so useful. And he was like, "feel discomfort and do it anyway, just embrace it, you have to embrace discomfort if you want to progress in your career, you just have to get comfortable with feeling really uncomfortable sometimes".'

What is so inspiring in Iris's example is that it clearly demonstrates the impact people in senior positions can have on others when they are willing to be vulnerable. Sadly, I hear many employees say they fear showing that level of vulnerability, believing it can only come from the person at the top. However, an organisation that has a culture of vulnerability and openness can have a positive impact on those working within that organisation.

Do you feel your organisation is supportive? Or do you think the organisation or those at the top are paying lip service or even pretending to provide support? Perception is reality – if you don't perceive the support to be there, it isn't. But an environment in which employees perceive support and feel psychologically safe can help reduce imposter feelings, reduce stress levels and consequently increase productivity.[4]

Several people I interviewed spoke about the positive impact that a supportive workplace culture can have, especially one that values humility and compassion, and provides mental health support. Here are short extracts from Amy, Ben and Quinn's interviews.

Amy: 'There is an underlying culture in the organisation of humility.'

Ben: 'The bank has been really good from a mental health aspect and there's lots of information out there for us.'

Quinn: 'I think now we're starting to get a bit more used to a culture of "let's be compassionate, we're not robots". And "do your best, but you need to take some downtime".'

Some people work for organisations that they feel only pay lip service to their stated values. However, Quinn highlighted that an organisation's values can be encouraging. One organisation he had previously worked for had declared values of 'being courageous and putting yourself forward'. Quinn tries to live up to this principle and act in circumstances where he feels uncomfortable saying to himself, 'right, I'm going to do this and, yeah, it's scary.'

Another of my participants, Amy, emphasised the positive impact of the support she receives from her organisation and the beneficial effect this has had on her willingness to be open and vulnerable with colleagues. Amy's observations reflect research findings on the positive impact of receiving external support, which has been found to increase self-confidence, inspire hope and sustain courage.[5]

Jean described her supporters as 'cheerleaders' and suggested that we all need different cheerleaders for different parts of our lives. Jean also said that although in her experience women are very good at building networks, she questions whether they are good at using these networks for support when needed. Whether this is a gendered issue is a moot point; regardless of gender, many people tell me that they think asking for support seems 'weak' or 'needy'. It isn't, and I would encourage everyone to heed the words of the horse in Charlie Mackesy's book, to be brave and ask for help.

Finding your cheerleaders or external support may also help drown out internal negative thoughts. Mark, a broker in his fifties, said that having support from others bolstered his internal courage: 'I think it's incredibly helpful to have external reassurances to help you drown out the negative internal voices. And, if they're there, perhaps you have the courage to say, "don't be silly" to yourself and tell the internal voices to "do one".'

Having someone offer support also helps put doubts into perspective. Such support helped me many times during my own research. Especially when I would start to doubt myself and look for reasons to stop my studies, wondering how I could give up as I was sure that I could not write a PhD thesis, let alone pass a viva examination. Yet, my supervisors kept encouraging me to keep going. Without their support, I may have given up, and my PhD would certainly have been an even more stressful experience.

External support has also been found to be beneficial for leaders. Researchers at an American university interviewed 29 women in leadership positions and concluded that the majority did not feel like imposters. Their confidence levels were attributed to mentors, romantic partners and support from other women in leadership positions.[6]

Support, whether from colleagues, role models, mentors or romantic relationships, was highlighted in my research. In this excerpt from my interview with Gail, when her imposter fears reared their head and she started to doubt herself and her capabilities, it was her husband who gave her support:

> 'I found myself in front of a spreadsheet, I was sat by myself in the kitchen because it was a very small company, so it was just me, at home, working for them. And I didn't understand really what was being asked of me and I didn't have anybody to fall back on or ask any questions. So I burst into tears, and I just thought "I've done something wrong here, I've made a mistake, I am not the person that I made myself out to be in the interview, not capable enough, I need to just phone my bosses and just tell them that I've made a mistake, they've made a mistake." Thankfully, my husband saw me; he said "Take a deep breath, you wouldn't have been offered the job if you weren't good enough".'

Mentors are also effective providers of external support. One of my participants described a mentor as 'somebody to whom you can go and ask for advice on things'. Many organisations have formal mentoring programmes where employees can be matched with suitable mentors. Informal mentoring is also really effective, where you casually meet for a cuppa. Sometimes the other person doesn't even realise you see them as a mentor.

Role models also provide support and encouragement. As Kelly succinctly put it: 'For me, seeing other women doing similar things and leading the way is what really encourages me. It gives me courage to go and do things.' Dawn described the impact and importance of being a role model for others at work: 'I still don't feel like a role model (laughs). I mean, I know I am. I've learned the power of leadership, the privilege in the job is you're being watched all the time, and I know there are younger women that have said, "I just want to be like you" and I used to think, "why the hell do you want to do that!" I didn't respond like that, obviously . . . but I wear it [role model] lightly.'

A contradiction on role models came from Lisa when, during her interview, she highlighted the tension that can exist between what a female role model says and what she does: 'We're on that cusp of a generation where we were brought up being told you can be whatever you want to be. But our mums were all still at home looking after us. So you have the home-keeper as your role model; is that what you should be doing? That's what you're brought up with, so you make assumptions about a woman; mum is at home, looking after children and keeping the house really nice.'

Time in

- -

- Who is your mentor?
- How often do you meet with them?
- Have you a role model?
- What is it about them that inspires you?

- -

'If you can't see the role model, be the role model.'

Kate Atkin

Belonging and otherness

As covered earlier, many organisations have EDI policies and pro-grammes in place that focus on equality (or equity), diversity and inclusion. While these programmes aim to promote a sense of belonging in the workplace, the EDI agenda cannot fully capture the complex nature of developing a sense of belonging.[7] As we have seen, imposter feelings can be exacerbated by a feeling of not belonging or a sense of otherness. This otherness or lack of belonging can come from many directions. For instance, it may depend on whether the work environment feels inclusive, your perception of societal expec-tations or whether you feel you are going against expectations. It can also stem from an absence of role models or from the underrep-resentation of, for example, people of different gender, sexuality, dis-ability, age, race, ethnicity or socioeconomic backgrounds (this is not an exhaustive list). While the EDI agenda can be helpful in address-ing some of the reasons for otherness, there is still a way to go in the workplace to create a sense of belonging for everyone.

As mentioned at the start of this chapter, the simple act of having conversations with other people about imposter feelings can reduce the associated stress and anxiety[8] and help with the realisation that the imposter phenomenon is a 'thing', that you are not 'weird', nor is it a 'quirk' (all words used by my interviewees). Normalising imposter feelings can increase a sense of belonging and help sep-arate the thinking from reality, which is part of a coping strategy. In Ellie's words: 'I think the awareness of what it is has made a big difference to me in terms of the [imposter] chatter. I don't know that it's reduced, but it has helped me manage it more.' Harbouring negative beliefs about the self can also be detrimental to produc-tivity and mental well-being.[9] However, while knowing you are not alone in having imposter thoughts can be beneficial, in my view it is not enough. In the next chapter I discuss not just how to cope with imposter thoughts, but strategies that may reduce them.

A sense of otherness at work, of not belonging alongside col-leagues, may also be linked with a perception of not having the 'right' qualifications. Several people I interviewed said they had the right skills and experience to do their jobs but felt that they did not have the right qualifications. This led to a feeling that they didn't really belong in that role and a concern that they might be found out.

Qualifications also contributed to this sense of not belonging and otherness. Specifically, a lack of qualifications, either not having the usual formal qualifications for the job, being underqualified, or being qualified in the 'wrong' field, was seen as a problem by a number of my research participants. This was despite them having the skills and experience to do the job and receiving feedback that they were doing it well. Simply having the skills, knowledge and experience was not sufficient to combat their imposter thoughts.

Another aspect of qualifications highlighted by some of my participants was the need to acquire more qualifications than necessary; perhaps to compensate for feeling as if they did not belong and to help 'mask' their imposter thoughts. The extra qualifications and additional ad-hoc learning were often explained away as a 'love of learning' – a description I have used myself.

Here are some of the comments from my research participants relating to qualifications.

Ben: 'I'm not particularly qualified for the IT industry. I haven't got any formal qualifications, but I kind of learned skills in my previous role which then led me to be able to get this job. I'm underqualified and feel like I have flitted between roles . . . I've never really had an underlying qualification.'

Ellie: 'My first degree is in psychology, then I did my masters in risk management, but it was healthcare risk management. Yeah, the qualification set that I've got could be a lot stronger.'

Gail: 'I have no qualifications: I didn't finish college. I didn't go to university. I do have one business and admin qualification, but that was just like a free course. So, in terms of qualifications, I have absolutely nothing!''

▶

Lisa: 'Everybody's talking about what university they went to and what degree they've got and then you're going to have to say, "Huh, not me. Just the local comprehensive school!" It doesn't matter that you know what you know; that you've been doing the job for 30 years and they've only been doing it for 5. They're all so well educated.'

Tina: 'Two years ago, I did a Level 3 qualification, which is an A-Level equivalent, in digital marketing. In the wider team I have graduates that have, not even marketing degrees, but have marketing as part of their degree, a business degree, for example. And I still compare myself to them whereas I've done something that purely focused on marketing, they've done a wider degree. I still think that I'm not qualified – and I am!'

And here are some of the comments relating to being overqualified:

Simeon: 'Part of the reason I feel comfortable doing the job I do is I feel technically overqualified. My CV has every conceivable qualification I could have for my role on it already.'

Quinn: 'I've probably got more qualifications than other people at the HR business partner level. So, yeah, I don't want to sound conceited, but that's a good level of qualifications.'

Iris: 'I do tend to lean on and take a lot of comfort from doing additional qualifications and training to help me validate, partly for myself, my own capabilities.'

Time in

- Do any of the comments on qualifications resonate with you?
- How knowledgeable and skilled are you for your role?
- How qualified do you think you are?
- How qualified are you really?

As we have seen, the corporate or organisational environment can trigger imposter feelings, creating a sense of otherness or not being part of the group. As mentioned earlier, one reason for this can be how you feel you are represented regarding gender, ethnicity and other protected characteristics. However, there are other reasons, some of which may not be obvious. Quinn highlighted that if you have a different employment contract from your colleagues, this may also create a sense of being an outsider. He was on a fixed-term contract, not a permanent staff member, 'I'm not part of the normal furniture, if you like. So there's a feeling of exclusion.'

A sense of otherness may also arise if you have an introversion preference and perceive others around you as extroverts. As Iris explains: 'The overall culture and feel of where I work, I would say, as a general rule, it's quite an extroverted organisation. We have a lot of insurance brokers and, not that all insurance brokers are extroverted, but I would think that probably a good proportion have that preference in terms of how they spend their time and what their role is about. So sometimes I feel different in terms of how I show up and what my style is. And I feel like through not saying as much, or being a bit shy, or communicating slightly differently, I don't always feel like I completely kind of fit in.'

'Otherness' might also develop if you are a single parent, have a council house (social housing) upbringing, or when those around you went to public (i.e. private) school but you were state educated. Tina illustrated this when she commented: 'I'm not trying to say I'm a huge outlier, but I'm a single mum, I live in council house, I'm not a graduate, and I don't fit that mould of what people expect.' For Tina, her sense of not belonging also extended to friendships outside of the workplace: 'I know they're my very best friends and I could speak to them about anything, it's just, sometimes, I just kinda feel that I don't fit in. I'm in a council house and I don't I think any of my friendship group are, I think they all have mortgages.'

Sometimes a sense of not belonging comes from a completely unexpected source. For Dawn it was the size of her office: 'I can remember being shown to the most enormous office and someone telling me it's mine, thinking, "what the hell am I doing here?"'

Parents and family members can also unwittingly cause imposter thoughts, sometimes in the well-meaning way they express admiration for your achievements. This was highlighted by Lisa, whose parents kept saying to her: "'Gosh, I can't believe you're working in the City. I can't believe you're doing this." The more people say, "I can't believe it," all you're thinking is, "well, I can't believe it either" because someone's gonna realise I shouldn't be here!'

Societal expectations can also exacerbate imposter thoughts. In addition to a lack of role models, many of the women I spoke to were acutely aware of societal expectations about how women should behave and what they should be doing by a certain age. Organisations must definitely do more to create a sense of belonging for everyone. Changes in societal attitudes should help along the way, but it will take time, like turning the metaphorical tanker around.

Time in

- What is your workplace culture like? Is there a sense of belonging?
- What can you do to help create a sense of belonging for everyone?
- What or who helps you feel like you belong?
- What is the length of experience you have in your current role?
- Do you believe you have the knowledge, skills and experience to do your job?

In an interview after winning an Oscar in 2017, the actress Viola Davis alluded to a sense of not belonging and not deserving of success when she said: 'At 51 years old, I have a lifetime of experience. I've been doing this for over 30 years professionally. It feels like my hard work has paid off but, at the same time, I still have the imposter syndrome. I still feel like I'm gonna wake up and everybody is going to see me for the hack I am. I still feel like when I'm walking on set that I'm starting from scratch, until I realise I'm human. I know I'm not the best, but I'm proud of myself. This is the first year I've allowed myself, just a little bit, to see that, to realise that *self-deprecation is not the answer to humility. That sometimes you can say "I deserve it"*; that I'm proud of myself and move on.'[10]

This was Viola Davis's third Oscar! How many Oscars do you need to realise that you are good at your job? Of course, most of us won't win such high accolades but, even so, isn't it time to accept that you do belong and that you really are good at your job?

Donning armour

Another way to cope with imposter feelings is to arm yourself and be ready for 'battle' with your imposter thoughts. Or at least that was how some of my research participants described their coping techniques. Battling inner negative thoughts and being driven by a fear of being judged negatively are associated with imposter feelings,[11] and arming themselves to avoid that negative judgement was paramount for some of the people I spoke to, including Gail:

> 'They battle each other constantly, don't they? You've got your courageous side wanting to come forward and speak up in that meeting; you want to be the one to ask that question; you want to be the one to come up with a very valid point. But the imposter syndrome says to you, "this is a very important meeting with people from America and, you know, they're big leaders, what if you ask the wrong question, what if it sounds stupid?" So that is constantly an internal battle.'

So what did this armour look like? Well, for most of the participants who used battle terminology, it took the form of preparation. Obviously some preparation is necessary before meetings, presentations and other important events. However, a fear of negative judgement drives some people to over-prepare. Remember Cleo from the previous chapter, who wanted to triple or even quadruple-check her facts before she contributed to a discussion at work? Has that also been you?

Another of my participants, Kelly, talked about the extent to which she went when preparing for a speech, even learning it word for word, because, in her words, 'I was determined that I would do my best and not give anybody a reason to kick me down.' As Nina put it, the point of preparation was to give her 'peace of mind. So, if something goes wrong, it's not my fault, it's not on me, I've done everything.'

If this level of preparation is what helps someone cope with their imposter feelings, is it actually a bad thing?

Well, it may be . . .

Preparation comes with a considerable cost in terms of time and personal energy.[12] In addition, perfectionistic tendencies, which often go hand in glove with preparation, can increase imposter feelings.[13]

Lisa: 'You can't let that side of you win, you've got to keep facing your fears and covering up your feelings of not being quite good enough.'

Roger: 'It's a constant battle between "Yes, I do actually know what I'm doing" and "Oh, god, they're gonna find me out".'

Although preparation was used as a coping strategy, a few participants acknowledged that it was not always a positive way to cope. Over-preparing can contribute to missing deadlines and also cause burnout.[14]

Overworking tasks may also have a negative impact on the outcome and be an inappropriate use of time.[15] This was certainly the case when I was writing my second academic essay for my master's degree. I had been awarded a distinction for my first ever academic essay, so I decided to aim for a distinction for *every* essay. That meant extra work, reading more articles, citing more references, working longer hours and reworking the essay structure over and over again. The result? I 'only' achieved a merit in my next essay, despite all the extra effort I had put in. I was extremely disappointed. Although a merit was more than 'good enough', and a pass was all I really needed, I had failed my own standards. My imposter thinking kicked in and said that that first distinction must have been a fluke and was undeserved.

Sometimes it is possible to achieve more by working less. This realisation had occurred to a couple of my participants, who described how, having reduced the time they spent preparing, they were now more willing to go with the flow. As Holly reflected, 'over the decades of my career, I have stopped being a detailed person' because the level of detail would either be unnecessary or the information could be found out later. Quinn was inspired to stop over-preparing by a discussion with a technical manager at a former workplace, 'if he'd gone to the nth degree, nothing would ever get done. And it made me realise that sometimes you've just got to go for it.'

Another way of arming themselves against imposter feelings used by my participants was to look at what could go wrong and assess the worst-case scenario before deciding what action to take. This is something psychologists term defensive pessimism.[16] Assessing worst-case scenarios, mentally running through everything that could go wrong and lowering expectations of the outcomes help put things in perspective. Sometimes it is much better to try and stop ruminating like this and take action: to 'just do it'.

Dawn: 'I think, as I've got older, it's about a sense of perspective. Whether it really matters. I'm not a brain surgeon you see, I'm not saving people's lives.'

Iris: 'For me it's embracing feeling a bit uncomfortable and just doing it, and trying to challenge myself and be like, come on, what's the worst that can happen?'

Quinn: 'I always think, what happens if it goes wrong? What's the worst that can happen? Ok, you might be embarrassed in front of people. You might get sacked. Well, you're not dead, you'll survive, you will keep going.'

Another piece of armour my participants spoke about was trying to build their resilience, although they mainly described it as developing grit and determination. Here's an excerpt from Quinn's interview:

> **'There will be collateral, there will be mistakes. You might feel terrible about things at times, you might make cockups . . . But you pick yourself up, you learn from it, you do better, you keep going and, if you fail, well, ok, fine. But you learn from it, then it's never a mistake.'**

Letting go of high expectations and lowering the armour a little was also seen as beneficial. For instance, Cleo has managed to reduce her expectations of herself – just a little:

> **'I do go through what I'm about to say a few times and try and do a quick sort of risk analysis and assess how sure I am that what I'm about to say is correct. I'm trying to lower the bar for confidence, so I don't have to be 99 per cent sure it's right. Now I'm trying to go with: ok, if I'm 80 per cent right, let's just say it.'**

Time in

- When do you tend to over-prepare?
- What could you do less of without compromising the result?
- Where could you practise this first? Maybe in the home environment?

Finding courage

A key focus of my research was to understand the role of courage in overcoming or coping with imposter feelings. In my research interviews, I introduced the concept of courage to my participants. This section discusses their reactions.

But first, what do we mean by the word 'courage'? The concept of courage has long been debated by philosophers. Many have tried and failed to agree on a definition, going as far back as Socrates who debated the nature of courage with Athenian generals[17] and failed to reach a conclusion. The etymology of the word courage provides some insight into actions that are deemed to be courageous. The classical Greek word for courage is *andreia* (manly, brave), while the Latin word is *fortitude* (strength). Both imply a military association. In contrast, the French-English word courage is derived from the French *coeur*, meaning heart and provides an insight into the idea that there is more to courage than brave actions in conflict situations.[18]

Like the cowardly lion in *The Wizard of Oz*,[19] my participants did not see themselves as courageous. At first, many dismissed the idea of being courageous. However, through our discussions there was a growing recognition that they had, indeed, acted courageously, both in past situations and in the present. Research indicates that courage is often recognised only after the event through reflection.[20] It was this act of reflecting during the interviews that helped my participants realise that they had been brave and that they do possess courage.

The cowardly lion was awarded a medal for his courage by the wizard; similarly, Iris recounts the positive impact of being nominated for an industry award (but she also finds another reason for her nomination): '[the nomination] serves an organisational reputational purpose in that it's good for organisational profile and I can totally get the strategy behind it. So it's not all about me but, at the same time, it's really helped me, as actually I think it does indicate some recognition of what I have been contributing recently.'

Several participants suggested that being described as courageous 'sounded wrong', or they thought of courage as undertaking 'heroic actions', which did not apply to them. They preferred to distance themselves from being courageous, instead describing their actions as dutiful and the result of situations in which they 'just had to' act.

Here, I am talking about psychological courage rather than the more familiar physical courage that is a willingness to act in the face of a life-threatening situation. Psychologists define psychological courage, or 'inner courage' as I sometimes term it, as the 'courage to face our irrational fears and anxieties'.[21] Psychological courage refers to acts that are psychologically difficult and challenging for the individual but that may be invisible to others.

The realisation of the difference between everyday actions as seen by others and what happens on the inside was expressed by Lisa: 'Internally, I feel it takes a lot of courage for me to turn up at events and appear confident. But I'm not sure anyone else around me would think that's courage. Instead, they'd just think "why is she so pathetic? It's just normal life that everyone has to go meetings and stand up and do those things," and not realise that, actually, it's often quite hard for people to do it.'

The VIA Character Strengths Inventory,[22] a free online tool to help individuals identify their core character strengths, defines courage as a virtue that includes the strengths of honesty, bravery, perseverance and zest. In examples of courageous actions given by my participants, they used words such as 'bravery', 'gumption', 'stubbornness', 'digging deep', 'doing the unexpected' and 'willingness to place the fight bet'. Many of my participants used fight and battle terminology when describing courage, similar to fighting and battling with their imposter thoughts that I mentioned earlier. There was a reluctance to use the word courage, perhaps indicating that the term courage is felt to be too high an accolade for individuals experiencing imposter thoughts to accept.

Here is what courage meant to Fay, Ellie and Gail:

Fay: 'Holding yourself accountable to your own values and having the gumption to do that. Courage is the strength to pull back to those values, to then ask: am I upholding them to myself?'

Ellie: 'For me, it is quite literal. It's digging in, trying to keep the blinkers on and not look sideways whilst I'm dealing with what's ahead of me.'

Gail: 'It's fighting against that fight or flight response. Taking a deep breath and really putting some effort in.'

Gail also described her courage as rooted in her childhood experiences: 'I think when you've had the childhood and the teenage years that I had and the experiences that I had, you can't really get much worse. So courage for me is it can't really get much worse than what I've already been through. So you've got to take those chances, you've got to put yourself out there . . . you've just got to do it.'

The context or environment also impacts whether a person or an action is considered courageous. An external observer of the action, or someone who knows the situation, can help an individual recognise and acknowledge an act as courageous.[23] However, psychologically courageous actions are usually invisible to others, so this external recognition may be lacking. As a result, psychologically courageous acts may not be acknowledged by either the actor or an observer. This is illustrated by Kelly, who recalls the difficulty in seeing her actions as courageous: 'I must have had some [courage] to be able to move through it [imposter phenomenon]. And it would have been important, but I'm just not sure whether I categorise it as courage.'

Ben did not feel he used courage, yet he went on to recount an internal battle between courage and his imposter, with the imposter winning:

> 'The imposter overpowers my internal courage, definitely. Outside of the workplace in actual, almost life-threatening situations, I can take control and I've got lots of courage. But in the workplace the imposter overpowers, almost controls the situation and says, "yeah, you shouldn't be here, you don't deserve to be, you've not done anything to actually achieve this".'

Roger viewed courage as heroic actions and had not considered the role of internal courage:

> 'Courageous to me just seems more about the heroic stuff . . . um, I've never really thought about it as being an internal thing.'

Una describes using a mask instead of courage to avoid showing her true feelings:

> 'So to me, it always feels more of a mask rather than internal courage. Where I'll try and use humour to get people on a friendlier basis, particularly when it's a situation that I don't know people and I'm feeling quite intimidated.'

While courage was difficult for participants to define and describe, the following quote from Tina shows how thinking about courage during the interview prompted reflection and reframing:

> 'It's nice to have a label. It's actually made me look at it quite differently. It's nice to know that, when I'm stuck in a rut or the washing up's not done, or whatever, that little spark that says "get out there" is courage; and I really like that . . . I don't think I will ever be in a place, no matter

how many years into my career, that I would not feel like that. But I've got courage now which I didn't have until an hour ago. I know that it is about labels and knowing now that I have the label of courage to do it . . . it's a great word (chuckles). It's a great word. I think, yeah, having that word there has made a difference to how I'm going to view doing things now. Yeah, it's been a good week!'

So like the lion in *The Wizard of Oz*, many of my participants realised on reflection that they had had courage all along; they just hadn't labelled it as such. Labelling actions as courageous can help you recognise when you have used courage, and research indicates that this increases the likelihood of more courageous acts in the future.[24]

Time in

- When have you acted courageously?
- When have you used psychological (inner) courage?
- What inspired you to act in those circumstances?
- How would you describe your actions in terms of courage now?

chapter 7

How can I get rid of my 'imposter'?

'Not everything that is faced can be changed. But nothing can be changed until it is faced.'

James Baldwin, *As Much Truth As One Can Bear*

I believe it takes courage to overcome your imposter feelings; it also requires a different type of thinking. It can be easy to self-deprecate, to downplay your achievements so you don't appear arrogant, and to stay safe 'in your lane' and not make the most of your own potential. Taking a more positive view of yourself and owning your strengths and achievements is not straightforward. It takes courage to rethink how you see yourself and to believe that you are worthy of your achievements. It takes courage to accept deep inside that you have developed knowledge, skills and abilities that you didn't have before and to be comfortable with who you are now.

In the previous chapter, we saw examples of the common misconception that preparation helps reduce imposter feelings. While preparation is needed for that meeting we are about to attend, for the presentation we are about to give, and for that decision we want to challenge, the key is not to over-prepare. To be good enough, not perfect.

As mentioned in Chapter 4, imposter feelings are often coupled with a desire to be perfect and can drive over-preparation.[1] Over-preparing can also make you mistakenly think that any successful result has only been achieved because of the effort you put in. This could mean that you attribute successes to effort rather than to your skills or experience, thereby externalising the reasons for successes. On the other hand, failures may be attributed to internal factors and can be over-generalised.[2] Simeon sums up the impact of failures and successes by saying: 'I'll feel a success for an hour or a day; failure I'll feel for a week or a month.'

Perfection, though unattainable, is still often aimed for. Below are some of the comments made by my participants, which indicate the extent of the preparation they undertook and the lengths they went to in order to be 'perfect'. Although they saw it as a coping strategy, I don't think this is an effective strategy. Imagine how much time, energy and effort they spent, much of which was not necessary or productive.

Gail: 'I'm fully aware that, if I don't prepare, then I'm allowing myself to fail, and that being prepared is the most important part of success.'

Lisa: 'Being very well prepared before you go [to a meeting]. So you've researched pretty much everything that you can.'

Nina: 'It's preparation, preparation, preparation. Then where are you going, who are you meeting, what's the tone of the meeting, what's the objective, and have everything in place.'

Quinn: 'So courage is one thing but, if you plan ahead and anticipate and work out your coping strategies in advance, you don't need to be courageous because you've planned ahead.'

Una: 'I was literally the proper geek, I printed off the regulations and I read them. Nobody actually reads them, but I read them, and I put little tabs in. I knew them to a point where I could say "I think that's chapter da-da".'

One of the most memorable comments on preparation came from Simeon, who would spend a day preparing for a one-hour meeting:

'Research every possible branch of the tree that you might go down and have an answer prepared. I prepare, over-prepare, so thoroughly that I'm never blindsided; I'm literally unblindsidable.'

It is important to remember that imposter feelings are dependent on the situation. For example, you may experience deeply troubling imposter feelings at work yet feel completely comfortable in another environment. Speaking up in meetings at work, asking questions or challenging a decision when you don't believe you have the right to be there is very different from, say, helping out at a local community group. In one case, you might feel like everyone else is more knowledgeable than you; in the other, it might feel more like being among friends and equals.

So the glib answer to how someone can get rid of their imposter feelings is to just get out of the situation that causes them. This may be flippant, but it emphasises that the imposter phenomenon is not a mental health condition and doesn't follow a person around in the way that anxiety or depression can.

Some people give up very good careers to reduce the stress caused by their imposter feelings or turn down promotions because they don't feel they deserve them. If feeling like an imposter results from a successful career, even though you may not think that you deserve that success, it is indeed well deserved; it is not a fluke, a one-off or a mistake. Reducing stress levels by changing jobs is the right decision for some people. However, since you are reading this book, I am guessing you would rather reduce your imposter feelings to reduce the stress, than change jobs or careers.

This chapter covers the effective strategies mentioned by my participants and a few other strategies researchers have identified for coping with imposter feelings, reducing them, and maybe eliminating them. There is much more research needed into this area. Despite some advice you may read online, it is not an overnight fix. There are no quick wins. It takes time, effort and some discomfort. But the end result of being free of the stress and anxiety caused by feeling like an imposter is worth it.

Read on, test the different strategies and see what works for you.

Knowing about the imposter phenomenon

Researcher Joel Lane conducted interviews at Portland State University with 29 young adults who were transitioning from university to the workplace.[3] He saw his participants express a sense of relief when, during the interviews, they realised that their imposter feelings were a 'thing', that they were not alone, and that it wasn't just them who felt that way. Being able to name your feelings as the 'imposter phenomenon' can be very helpful. As my participant Nina said, 'the problem is sometimes you can't even name the problem.' Knowing and naming the feelings as the imposter phenomenon is, in itself, a helpful coping strategy – a little like the ancient folktale of Rumpelstiltskin, whose power is removed once his name is discovered. The power of imposter feelings is reduced once you have a name for them.

Mark described hearing about the imposter phenomenon for the first time: 'It felt like a lightbulb moment. "Oh, that's what it was!" I'd felt it in the past but not been able to put a word to it.'

Holly felt a sense of relief when she learned about the imposter phenomenon: 'I came across this some years ago, and went "oh, my goodness, thank goodness there's actually a name for it and it's not just me." It was almost liberating because I thought, actually, if most people feel like that, then I'm not weird.' Liberating, reassuring and cathartic are all words that have been used by participants in my workshops when they realise that there is a name for feeling like an imposter.

Talk about it

I can remember going on stage at a national conference as a keynote speaker to talk about the imposter phenomenon in public for the first time. Was I nervous? Yes, absolutely. But the response from the audience afterwards was so encouraging. People who had known me for years in my role as a professional speaker were surprised to hear that I felt like an imposter. Speaking that day about my inner feelings of insecurity, wondering when I would be found out, and feeling not good enough led to many interesting, open and vulnerable conversations. It also led to me feeling less like an imposter. Once you have let your 'imposter' out of the bag, there is no going back. It was a huge relief not to worry about being found out anymore.

When you start to speak up about your inner imposter thoughts, it helps to encourage others to do the same. So it can have a double benefit: on you and those around you. As my participant Dawn said when speaking about her imposter thoughts: 'It feels liberating. Not in a gung-ho kind of way, but it just makes me feel like I'm being me. I find I feel very alive. Other people, a lot of people actually, just seem massively relieved someone said something.'

You're not alone

When you begin to talk about your imposter feelings, you start to realise that you are not alone. This was Ben's experience. He volunteered to participate in my study after attending a workshop on the imposter phenomenon organised by his employers. He said: "After having been on the conference call, I definitely learned a lot from that; I realised that a lot more people are going through what I am. That was a great help."

As I mentioned in Chapter 2, research indicates that 70 per cent of people may experience imposter feelings at some point in their working lives.[4] However, until we are more open about these feelings, they can make us feel isolated. It may seem simple, but knowing you are not the only person to feel this way and that it is a common occurrence can be really beneficial in lessening the intensity of the feelings.

Personify it

Ellie personifies her imposter and separates it from herself. She says: 'Personifying the voice and thinking of it in the corner as a goblin helps.'

For many years I have had a book on my shelves called *Taming Your Gremlin* by Richard Carson.[5] Among other tips, the book encourages readers to recognise their gremlins – that inner voice that undermines your confidence and raises self-doubt. The objective is to observe self-sabotaging thoughts and use mindfulness to 'tame them'. Observing and maybe naming your 'imposter gremlin', giving it a voice, perhaps a silly squeaky one, or giving it its own persona, may help lessen the intensity of the imposter feelings.

Don't fake it until you make it

'Fake it until you make it' is advice often given to those who want to build their confidence. And it can be a useful strategy in those situations. But if you are experiencing imposter thoughts, I think it is the wrong advice. You may feel as if you are faking it but, when you are genuinely experiencing imposter thoughts rather than normal self-doubt, you will already have a track record of success. In other words, you have already made it. Yet the inner imposter thoughts are telling you otherwise, so you *think* you are still faking it. That's why 'fake it until you make it' won't work to reduce imposter feelings. You need to realise that you are *not* faking it.

However, putting on an act and 'pretending' to be something other than the perceived self is common when experiencing imposter feelings. Here, Jean talks about how she wants to be perceived in the office and how she creates that impression:

'I want to be perceived as a senior woman with a career going places who knows stuff, has answers, that's how I want people to see me. That's how I act in the office. But it's not me really. I stalk around the office in my heels and my red dress, with my head held high. I'm projecting utter confidence, that's all! Actually, I want to slink in and sit at the corner. I will walk into the room where I'm presenting, and I will find a seat in the middle, and I'll be wearing nice clothes, and I'll be sat confidently with my head up talking assertively. And it's all an act.'

Yet is Jean really acting or just thinking that she is still acting? Jean is in her mid-fifties and holds a senior management position. Her knowledge, skills and abilities are significant. Maybe in the past she was faking her confidence, but now?

We are prone to comparing ourselves to others rather than examining our growth over time. By doing so, we can perpetuate the illusion that we are still 'faking it'. Instead, accept that you have 'made it'.

Stop comparing yourself to others

Comparing ourselves to others is known to exacerbate feelings of the imposter phenomenon. If you look hard enough you will always be able to find someone better than you, with more experience than you, and with more knowledge than you. Stop looking and redirect your energy to something more worthwhile and supportive.

Here's another quote that I love from Charlie Mackesy's book *The Boy, The Mole, The Fox and The Horse*:

> **'"What do you think is the biggest waste of time?" asked the boy**
>
> **"Comparing yourself to others," said the mole.'**

Start comparing yourself to yourself

Stop comparing yourself to others and start to compare yourself to yourself. What do you know this week that you didn't know last week? What about this time last month? Last year? Our knowledge grows all the time, but we rarely take time to stop and reflect on how much we have learnt, how much we have changed, and how much we have developed.

Quinn reflects on his 'positive playlist' to help diminish his imposter thoughts. The idea being that, if he has already coped with those scenarios successfully (remember, it is a positive playlist, *not* a list of things that have gone wrong!), then he can cope with the current or forthcoming situation. It's a little like your own bespoke Spotify playlist, made up of your own positive real-life events to aid your self-comparison.

Here are Jean, Gail and Quinn discussing the benefits of comparing themselves to themselves and reflecting on how far they have come and what they have achieved:

Jean: 'The more things I tick off, the more I feel I have achieved and the progress that I've made. I'm able to look back and go: look, here's how far you have come.'

Gail: 'I was a single parent not very long ago with no job, living off benefits, so I think taking a step back and travelling back

---

> that far in time and thinking: you know, you had nothing going for you whatsoever and literally just got on with a bit of grit.'
>
> Quinn: 'So, I'm trying to think against my natural brain pattern. I'm trying to think: "Ok, let's be reflective on this and think more objectively about where your performance is, without ego getting in there".'

Remove your ego

Quinn's mention of the ego here is interesting. Most people I speak to who experience imposter thoughts do not consider themselves egotistical. In fact, I'd go as far as to say that they would hate to be seen that way. Yet there is some research that the imposter phenomenon is correlated with neuroticism[6] and even narcissism,[7] both of which are associated with the ego.

It is beneficial to get your ego out of the way and accept that you are good enough. We fear being judged negatively by others, we want to be liked, we fear making mistakes (even though that's how we all learn), we fear disagreements with others when we present our ideas, and we fear looking stupid. If our egos were in check, we would realise that many of these fears are irrational. Coaching, mentoring or support from your manager may help you gain this perspective.

An alternative comparison

Some of my participants used a different comparison. Instead of looking for people they thought were doing better than them, they looked for people who were not doing so well, but were still 'good enough'. They sought comparisons with people who were lacking some of the skills that they themselves possessed. By objectively assessing where the standard of 'good enough' lies and assessing themselves against others who are perceived by others as 'good enough', their imposter feelings lessened.

Amy: 'It's only when I look at my own network and whether they've stalled where they are, that I realise, "yeah, actually, you have come a long way, despite the fact that you are still not perfect".'

Dawn: 'I think as I've got older, I've learned that, actually, it's not always intellect that I am witnessing; it's bullshitting in some cases and a degree of self-importance. As they're actually probably not any brighter than me.'

Olivia: 'I remind myself how rubbish a lot of people are. What I try and do is, rather than tell myself this is the bar [gestures high] and I'm there [gestures lower], it's more like: you know what, my bar's here [gestures high] but the bar's probably here [gestures lower], and that's ok. It sounds a little bit negative in the sense that I bring people down to make myself feel better. I just think that the pressure you put on yourself is often unrealistic relative to what people's expectations are and, if I put the bar down here and I'm up here, brilliant!'

Nina spoke about her thought processes and her reflections when she was offered her first management role. She compared herself with her peers to assess whether she could do the job: 'This may sound very badly on me, but what I did is: "Ok, these are the people on the team, someone has to do it" and, in my head, I made a list of everyone and thought who could do it better than myself. And, not to say I was the only one, I was like, "yeah, I mean, from all the people here, I can do this".'

Time in

- Who could you compare yourself to?
- How can you assess where the standard of 'good enough' really lies?

Try working to 80 per cent

Your imposter thinking is likely to cause you to overwork, perfecting tasks more than necessary. As mentioned earlier, this could involve colour-coding spreadsheets, aligning headings and fonts in a presentation, or checking the paragraph indentations on reports. What tasks do you tend to overwork?

Start by identifying a routine, non-critical task that you can do to, say, 80 per cent of your normal high perfectionistic standard. See if the impact of working to 80 per cent is as detrimental as you fear it might be. If lessening your standards to 80 per cent feels too much, then make incremental changes in what you reduce by starting to let something go when you are 95 per cent happy with it.

A while ago I found myself on a train home from London checking my emails, and a request for a guest blog post popped into my inbox. So I decided to write the blog while I was travelling. I sent it off about 30 minutes later and asked what else they needed. To my surprise, I received an email back saying that what I had written was exactly what was needed. Had I been at home I would have spent much longer writing and rewriting the article. In the end, it was just some quick tips that were used in the final article,[8] so perfecting the blog would have been a waste of time.

Sharing draft versions of your work can help you ascertain how much more input is needed. Using the word 'draft' as you share something also makes it seem less scary, as you are already intimating: 'This isn't perfect'. Any additions suggested by the reviewer or corrections they make will feel less like criticism and more like a helpful addition.

Putting extra effort in rarely reaps the rewards commensurate with the effort. It may make a marginal gain, which, if you are an Olympic athlete, could be the difference between gold and silver medals, so it is worth doing. But most of us are not Olympic athletes and, in the workplace, the mantra 'done is better than not done' is one that could be applied more often.

If testing working to 80 per cent out at work feels too big a leap, then start at home – maybe by doing some of the housework, gardening or cooking to 80 per cent of your usual standard. Then move on to applying it in the workplace.

Don't do your best

One of the reasons for the perfectionistic tendencies of many of my participants was their desire to *do* their best, not to *be* the best. This is contrary to a commonly held belief that those experiencing the imposter phenomenon want to be the best[9] and need to outperform others.[10] Here is Lisa talking about her efforts to do her best and the impact that has:

> 'There's a difference between being the best and wanting to do your best. And I don't care about being the best. I don't care about that, and I'm not competitive. I do care about doing my best. Somebody said to me at work that how I am about myself intimidates other people. Which I'm really sorry about because I think I'm the least intimidating person ever. Because I want everything to be done properly and I want everything to be done to the best that it can be – other people around me find that intimidating. They think that I am expecting that of everyone around me.'

Here's Quinn, with a rethink on doing his best:

> 'If I'm trying to "do my best", that means I work extra hard, because otherwise I'm not necessarily doing my best. And I'm now playing with that, because, actually, should we do our best? I'm thinking maybe we shouldn't, maybe we should just do what is enough. Is it good enough? Yes. Should we then stop, or do I have to keep overworking it?'

I have an issue with telling people, including children, to do their best. Doing your best encourages overwork and perfectionistic tendencies and applies extra pressure that doesn't need to be there. Crucially, how do you know when your best is done? There is always more that could be done. We only stop when we run out of time or energy. Lisa's example above gives a telling insight into the negative impact that doing your best all the time can have on those around you.

While saying 'do your best' is meant to be encouraging, it can create a fear of falling short of expectations. So what could be said instead? Perhaps take a leaf from Tal Ben-Shahar's work on perfectionism[11] and look to create an 'optimal' mindset. Ben-Shahar defines an optimal mindset as one that perceives failure as an opportunity for growth and not something to be feared. The optimal point is where the effort expended is enough to produce a worthwhile outcome, but no more. Any extra effort would not materially improve the outcome. Editing this book is important, but there is a point beyond which reworking and repositioning paragraph after paragraph and phrase after phrase is not going to make it any better (although, I am very tempted to keep trying!).

The Oxford English Dictionary defines 'optimal' as the 'best, most favourable, esp. under a particular set of circumstances'.[12] But 'do your optimal' sounds odd. So try saying: 'Do what you can within the time available.' At some point, we have to stop. The work is complete, the deadline has arrived or the book is written. Nothing would get done if we truly did our best every time.

Sometimes good enough really is just that: good enough.

Time in

- Where do you have a tendency to overwork?
- What can you let go of or do to 80 per cent?
- Who can you ask to review your first drafts?
- What would happen if you stopped aiming for perfection?
- How can you create an optimal mindset?

Build your resilience

Resilience is the ability to bounce back from adverse situations, as well as to keep going when things are going well.[13] Researchers in Germany found that an aspect of resilience, specifically play-fulness, may help reduce imposter feelings. A study with students and working professionals found that those high in 'light-hearted' playfulness were less likely to report imposter experiences.[14] The approach is one of creativity and enthusiasm,[15] transforming almost any situation into something amusing and entertaining through the imagination.

Perhaps this means we should not take ourselves so seriously. I know I tend to take other people's playful comments to heart and would benefit from not being quite so serious. In an attempt to bring more humour into my work and be more playful, I have been reading *Humour, Seriously* by Jennifer Aaker and Naomi Bagdonas,[16] lecturers at Stanford Graduate School of Business. The authors discuss the benefits that humour can bring, including enhancing communication skills, improving our connectedness to others and increasing our well-being. They suggest not looking for what is funny; instead, look for what is true, as that's where the humour lies.

While my participants did not specifically mention playfulness, they did speak about the positive impact of time passing, experience growing and learning to 'go with the flow'. They also mentioned mindfulness, which research shows also helps build resilience.[17] Tenacity, grit, determination, perseverance – whatever you call it, resilience can help you bounce back and carry on.

> Here Dawn and Gail describe their approach to being resilient:
>
> Dawn: 'So I've learned that I can actually deal with the issues. I pack them away, they're not permanently gone but I can pack them away. And I've learned that I'm actually more resilient doing that.'

> Gail: 'I think the kids for me are a massive motivation in terms of being successful, going through those struggles and showing that you can come through the other side . . . I'm much more resilient than I ever thought I was. It wasn't long ago where I just thought I was gonna be a waitress for evermore.'

Other participants used phrases that indicated they were practising mindfulness as a coping strategy without explicitly labelling it as such.

> Here are Dawn, Gail, Iris and Ellie who all spoke about breathing techniques:
>
> Dawn: 'Just go with the feeling, it's ok, just go with it, sit in it, sit in that feeling, it will be fine. And breathe, I mean literally breathe with the feeling, it's gonna be ok.'
>
> Gail: 'There's a little bit of a . . . to use the term ritual might be a bit too strong, but there's certainly things that you have, that are in place to prepare yourself, and then a couple of deep breaths to sort of, how would you describe that? Calm yourself? Ready yourself?'
>
> Iris: 'If I feel anxious I try and breathe more deeply into my diaphragm, which I find is quite useful. I take a few deep breaths and go "look, just let it play out a bit," and then it's fine.'
>
> Ellie: 'I've been really conscious of slowing my breath.'

In his interview, Quinn reflected on the battle with his imposter thoughts and spoke of a link between courage and resilience:

'I think it's probably a case of looking at some of the resilience, isn't it? Courage is one thing, but you will get beaten down at times, you will make mistakes, you'll get knocked about, things will happen to you . . . The courage piece is not necessarily avoiding those situations in the future but the courage piece is getting

back afterwards. And it's looking at the dialogue of what happened: Could I have done better? It's being honest with yourself about your mistakes. And it's about being beaten, but coming back later. So you might lose the battle, but you win the war.'

As Quinn says, there will be times when we feel beaten. But, if we are kind and compassionate towards ourselves, we will be able to get up and try again.

Practise self-compassion

Self-compassion is a factor in building resilience.[18] But what does it mean to be compassionate to oneself? Dr Kristin Neff has studied self-compassion for over 20 years. She suggests it has three main components: kindness (to the self rather than self-criticism), humanity (recognising the experiences of others, not being self-absorbed) and mindfulness (being aware of negative thoughts but not being attached to them).[19]

Researchers in Canada and Austria found lower levels of self-compassion among students who were experiencing intense imposter feelings.[20] They suggest that practising self-compassion may help to reduce imposter feelings. One way to do this might be through loving-kindness meditation or repeating a loving-kindness mantra.[21]

Self-talk is another factor in this act of kindness and compassion.

Watch your self-talk

In Chapter 1, I discussed the difference between imposter-style self-doubt and normal self-doubt, which is the lack of confidence we all feel when doing something new or when we don't have a track record of success. Paying attention to our inner conversations can help clarify this difference. Being aware of our self-talk can help us decide whether it is helpful, like that of a best friend, or if it is unhelpful.

Self-help books often discuss positive affirmations and how making upbeat statements to yourself can be helpful. A quick online search brings up a list of positive affirmations, including 'I am worthy of love', 'I am enough' and 'I am confident'. These may boost self-esteem and are useful for some people. Personally, I don't find this type of general self-praise very useful for controlling my imposter-style self-doubt.

Research has, however, identified the power of positive self-talk in coping with imposter feelings[22] and this strategy was also spoken about by my participants. The self-talk referred to by my participants was more personal than the positive affirmations above, and sometimes involved citing specific examples rather than generalisations. For example, Quinn's 'positive playlist' is a type of positive affirmation that gives him a confidence boost when he reviews it.

In other examples, Una encourages herself, saying: 'You can do it, come on, come on, you got it.' Roger noticed that he has started saying to himself: 'Actually, no: you are better than you think you are.' Kelly also tells herself: 'I am the best person for this regardless of my gender; I've proved myself.' And Iris has taken inspiration from podcasts that raised her awareness of how she talks to herself, while Pat reframes her experiences by 'taking time to step back' and asking herself: 'How can I reframe this? How can I think about it differently?'

Taking time, not only to talk positively to themselves inside their heads and to put matters into perspective, but also taking time to reflect on achievements, was a coping strategy used by Holly, Olivia and Lisa.

Here are extracts from their interviews:

Holly: 'So it was a little bit of a history of going back and saying, "But you've done lots of really difficult things before, you've skipped countries multiple times, you've changed jobs, you've worked in careers that were sideways moves into new careers and you just learned them as you went along". . . So there's a bit where you go again. That's kind of a track record.'

➤

Olivia: 'Whenever I feel that fear, that sense of anxiety in my tummy or in in my chest or wherever, it's about remembering that you've done this stuff before.'

Lisa: 'I think a lot of these things come with age and, the more times you face the situation, the less awful you feel about it. And you start to care a little bit less about people. So what if people think I don't know what I'm doing, the world is always about learning and it's ok to say, "I don't understand." Because if you say, "I don't understand," people will teach you and you'll learn more.'

Psychologists also suggest that positive self-talk can reduce self-handicapping behaviour and maladaptive perfectionism.[23] This could be done by reflecting on what constitutes 'good enough' according to objective standards. Or you could tell yourself some positive messages.

Here are some positive messages you might like to try:

- Good enough is good enough.
- Done is better than not done.
- Perfection is unrealistic and unattainable.
- Perfectionism is the enemy of good.
- I've done what I can within the time available.
- Just let it go or, as I like to say: 'Be more Elsa.'[24]

As mentioned in Chapter 1, over-thinking, rumination and anxiety may lead to an increase in imposter thoughts, so keep a close ear on your self-talk. Are you supportive or destructive in what you say to yourself? Often our self-talk could be much kinder and far less critical. I have heard many people suggest that, if our best friend spoke to us the way we speak to ourselves, we wouldn't have them as our best friend anymore. Is that true about the way you speak to yourself? Don't berate yourself for it. Observe the situation, and kindly note how interesting it is, perhaps even thank yourself for bringing it to your attention, and then adopt a curious mindset to see what you can do about it.

Give your confidence a boost

While feeling like an imposter is different from lacking self-confidence, giving yourself a confidence boost might help reduce your imposter feelings. Research with female doctoral students in an American university found that increased self-confidence was associated with lower-intensity imposter feelings.[25] So how can we do this ourselves?

One way is to reflect on your past positive experiences, which increases what psychologists call self-efficacy[26] – or self-confidence to you and me. In my book, *The Confident Manager*,[27] I propose creating a 'confidence wall' on which you write down specific memories of moments in time when you have done something that you feel good about. The idea is to draw a brick wall on a piece of paper, with each brick large enough to write in. Then in each brick, write one confidence-boosting achievement: one moment in time per brick. This builds a 'wall' of positive events that you can look at whenever you need a confidence boost. The wall is built from your own personal achievements, however grand or small they may be – and it is the small ones that often make the biggest difference.

The perspective used in this strategy is your own perspective of yourself, which is great for boosting your confidence. But to diminish imposter feelings, a different perspective is often needed. This is where the next strategy helps by seeking external evidence.

Find external evidence

In the original definition of the imposter phenomenon, Clance and Imes stated that people were feeling phoney *despite* the evidence of success.[28] Providing yourself with external evidence of your successes can help contradict and counteract your imposter thoughts. This evidence can be in the form of positive feedback. The key is to internalise your successes. In order to do this, I suggest there are three steps.

Step one: Keep your positive feedback

The first step is to keep your positive feedback. When feedback does not match your self-perception, it is easy to delete or ignore it. I suggest you start asking for and keeping positive feedback. This might feel very uncomfortable, so bear with me as I explain why.

To help cope with her feelings of not being good enough, Nina sought feedback from her team, which helped her realise that she was doing a good job as a manager. However, she needed external encouragement to ask for this feedback. In this case, it was her husband who persuaded her to look for facts rather than relying on her own perception of her abilities:

> 'He's a scientist and a very logical person. He's a mathematician, so one of his comments was, "how do you know you're not doing well?" Because it was just in my head, so I was not looking outside, and he was like, "how do you know? What are you basing that on?" I was like, yes, you're right, I need facts. So I started looking for information, and what's better information to know you're doing well as a manager than asking the people you're managing.'

Adverse events and negative feedback are remembered more clearly than positive events and positive feedback,[29] so we need to make extra effort to recall the positive.

The transient nature of positive feedback and the fleeting positive emotions resulting from successes were mentioned by Mark and Quinn:

Mark: 'I suppose it [positive feedback] made me think, well actually, maybe you can do bits of this job. Maybe you can do that bit. And I was fine on the journey . . . but once I got back to being at home, being alone and writing the notes up, it all came tumbling back down again.'

Quinn: 'So we have this 360-degree feedback process, and I got some really positive praise from other people. So that was good. But you don't always listen to it.'

By keeping the positive feedback you receive from others some-where specific, perhaps in a dedicated email folder, you are creating a collection of alternative, objective perspectives to reflect on – perspectives that may, in fact, be more accurate than your own. Some people have created 'smile files', 'brag files' and 'wonderful me' folders. My own folder is simply called 'feedback'. In the folder I suggest you store *all* the positive feedback you receive; you can photograph the feedback if it is on paper or type out a summary if it is a verbal comment and email it to yourself to keep in your folder. The important thing is to keep the feedback; don't dismiss it or delete it. External, objective evidence is a key component in overcoming imposter thoughts.

Step two: Regularly review your positive feedback

Keeping positive feedback is useful, but only if we look at it. There are some people who already keep their positive feedback in a folder but have never looked at it. To overcome imposter feelings, you need to look at it regularly. Suppose you only review your positive feedback, confidence wall, or replay your positive playlist when you need a boost, such as when applying for jobs, getting ready for your performance appraisal, or preparing for a presentation. In that case, the boost is short-term and helpful in that particular situation. However, to use positive feedback to overcome your imposter thoughts and feelings, the feedback needs to be reviewed more frequently. Maybe weekly, once a fortnight or at least once a month.

This can be a challenging exercise because, if you're like some of my participants (and me), looking at your positive feedback is extremely uncomfortable. As Nina says: 'I don't like praise; I feel like I have to just go under the table. I don't know how to react to it.' Or, in Ellie's words, it can be 'embarrassing to get good feedback'. But that is precisely why you are looking at it: to challenge your imposter thoughts with the external positive evidence provided by others. As you review your positive feedback, there is one more step to take . . .

Step three: 'Yes, and . . . ' your positive feedback

As well as keeping and reviewing your positive feedback, there is a third step I recommend you practise, which is to 'yes, and . . . ' your positive feedback as you review it. The idea is that this will help you to internalise it. This is an adaptation from theatrical improvisation – the art of making things up on the spot – something I have studied and practised during my self-development journey. In improvisation, one of the first rules that drama students are commonly taught is to say, 'yes, and . . . ' to keep the scene moving forward.[30]

Applying this principle to positive feedback means not allowing your imposter chatter to pop up and counter the feedback by saying, 'ah, but . . . ', 'you could have done it better', 'they're just saying that', 'what do they know?' To prevent that voice from appearing as you review your positive feedback, consciously add 'yes, and . . . ' at the end of the feedback. Quietly reflect on the feedback and say to yourself (not aloud!): 'Yes, and . . . I learnt [. . .] from that situation', or 'Yes, and . . . I can see my skills in [. . .] developing' or 'Yes, and this [. . .] is becoming a common theme, and it's now a strength of mine.'

So it is a three-step process to challenge your inner imposter thoughts with the external evidence:

1 Keep your positive feedback.

2 Regularly review your positive feedback.

3 'Yes, and . . .' your positive feedback.

Time in

- What inner conversations do you have when imposter feelings strike?

- Is your self-talk helpful? Or does it increase your imposter feelings and associated anxiety?

- Reflect on your inner conversations; practise self-compassion and kindness towards yourself.

- What could you say to yourself that would be helpful?

- Which phrases from the positive messages list could you try?

- What other phrases could you add to the list?

- Could you create a positive playlist, like Quinn?

- If you don't already have one, set up a dedicated email folder in which to keep your positive feedback.

- Set a reminder to review your positive feedback regularly and 'yes and . . . ' it when you re-read it.

Know and own your strengths

Knowing and using your strengths may help reduce your imposter feelings,[31] as well as give your mood a positive boost.[32] This is another area where more research would be useful, but collecting and reviewing your positive feedback will help you identify common threads and indicate your strengths.

If you are unsure of your strengths, as well as using feedback you could also opt to take an online strengths profile. One of my favourites is the Strengths Profile[33] developed by the Centre for Applied

Positive Psychology (CAPP). Alex Linley, co-founder of CAPP and author of Average to A+,[34] defines strengths as having three components:[35]

1 How you feel when you use them.
2 How often they are applied.
3 How successful are you at doing them.

Using this definition, a strength is something you are good at, something you get the chance to do and something you enjoy. It should incorporate all three areas. You can be skilled at doing something but, if it doesn't make you feel good or give you energy when you are doing it, then it is not classed as a strength.

This can be a lightbulb moment for some people, as it was for one of my workshop participants. She was working in a role that involved interacting with a lot with people. She was good at these interactions but, upon hearing the definition of a strength, she realised that just because she was good at something didn't mean she had to enjoy doing it. And she wasn't enjoying her job. That realisation started her thinking about a career change to one that better matched her strengths.

Knowing your strengths is one thing, but owning them is something else. Many people know what they are good at but, when I ask them to share a strength with others in workshops, they often downplay it, saying something like: 'Other people tell me I am good at . . .', or 'I think I am good at . . . ' instead of the more assertive statement: 'I am good at . . . ' It is also easy to opt to share a 'safe' strength such as listening, being a team player, or being good at communicating. Having a more detailed list of your strengths will give you yet more evidence to counteract your imposter thinking.

Reframe failure

When we make a mistake or fail at something, it is easy to be harsh towards ourselves. Logically we know that we learn from mistakes, yet we can strive very hard to avoid them. This sometimes means turning down new opportunities when they arise for fear of failing, or trying extra hard to ensure success, or working longer hours than necessary to reduce the chance of a mistake.

My desire to be 'perfect' meant that I interpreted making a mistake as meaning that I had failed in some way. In my head, mistakes confirmed that 'I was a failure'. There can also be a massive difference in our emotional reactions to successes and failures, as illustrated in this comment from Mark: 'I grieve failures much more than I celebrate successes.' Does that sound familiar to you? We are all human; we will make mistakes.

While researching for my master's degree, I had the pleasure of interviewing 12 successful entrepreneurs, men and women. When I asked about their failures and what happened, two of the twelve became animated and said that any failure or mistake, whether made by them or their team, was disastrous and they worried that they would be 'found out'. Unsurprisingly, these two entrepreneurs scored highly on the Clance Imposter Phenomenon Scale, reporting intense imposter feelings. But my real learning came from the other 10 entrepreneurs, who reported only mild imposter feelings. When asked the same question, there was often a long pause, and then came their response: they didn't recognise failure. Instead, they said that they had found a number of 'things that didn't work', had learnt from it, and moved on. Failure to them was not a big deal; it was not internalised. Instead, it was seen as a learning opportunity.

This idea of reframing failure struck me on an emotional level. Objectively, I had known for many years that we learn better from our failures than from our successes. But hearing 10 successful people describe their failures as 'things that didn't work' was really powerful. We could do well to reframe our failures in this way and to talk about what we have learned. Indeed, some teams and organisations have 'post-mortem' meetings to decipher what went wrong. By reframing mistakes as learning opportunities, these meetings could be even more powerful. Focusing on the lessons learnt would encourage people to speak up about their mistakes – sorry, learning opportunities.

Practise failing safely

In a meeting with my PhD supervisors, we came up with the idea that trying to deliberately fail at something might help reduce the fear of failure. What if we try to do something that we are not good at, something that doesn't really matter? Then we can learn in a safe way that not being good at something doesn't always have negative consequences. Learning to fail safely by finding things that 'didn't work', learning from it, and moving on might help reduce the fear of failure and reduce the linked imposter thoughts.

Until now there's been no research on this strategy, but you could try it out. Not at work though! Take up a hobby or do something you expect to fail at or even aim to do it badly. This could be something like learning a language or a musical instrument, painting, woodwork or maybe writing poetry.

One place that truly welcomes mistakes and even goes as far as embracing them is the theatre of improvisation, as discussed above with saying 'yes, and . . . ' to positive feedback. In improvisational theatre, often shortened to improv, players make up scenes, dialogue and characters on the spot, frequently incorporating ideas from the audience. I found that improv classes were a good vehicle for taming my desire to get things 'right' and encouraged me to go with my gut feeling. I learned that, in improv, the more things went 'wrong' (i.e. were unexpected), the greater the laughs. I realised that making mistakes could be a good thing and learned to be more comfortable with them.

Improv isn't everyone's idea of fun and might be your worst nightmare, but where can you play, get things wrong and be ok with the learning that comes from it?

Time in

- When have you failed at something?
- What happened? Who were you with?

- How did it feel at the time?
- How does it feel now as you reflect on the situation?
- What did you learn from that experience?
- Where can you learn to fail safely?

- -

Rewrite your story

We all have messages and stories that we repeatedly tell ourselves about ourselves. Sometimes these are factually correct but, as with most stories, some have been embellished over time, and some are no longer true or were not even true in the first place. We don't often spend time reflecting on our stories, but if they are inaccurate and fuelling our imposter thoughts, a rewrite could be very useful. It wasn't until my late forties that I reframed my 11-plus failure and began to rewrite my own story of not being clever or good enough. It came from the realisation that I am an August baby and that would have disadvantaged me when I sat the exam because I would have been younger than everyone else in my year. I was also much younger than my siblings were when they sat the same exam. So my failure may have been down to my age and development, and my comparison with my siblings was skewed.

Take time to reflect on your own imposter thoughts, collect and review the positive feedback from others, let go of the need to be perfect or right and practise doing things to 80 per cent of your normal high standard. Reflect on your own self-talk, review the childhood messages you were told and reframe failures as learn-ings. All these strategies, and more, will be helpful in reducing your imposter thoughts. They may also help you in rewriting your story to one that is more accurate and will serve you well in the future.

Maybe your story could incorporate the following:

- You are worthy (of the role).
- You will not be found out because you are already in the right place with the right skills.
- You are good enough (at your job).
- You are imperfect, and that is ok.

In the next chapter I discuss how you can use psychological courage to update the view you have of yourself to one that is more accurate and more positive.

chapter 8

Cultivating courage

'I've got courage now which I didn't have until an hour ago. It's been a good week!'

Tina, *research participant*

As I write this, in July 2024, the England football team is playing Switzerland in the European Championship. The match has just gone to a penalty shootout for a place in the semi-finals, and England player Bukayo Saka is lining up to take a penalty shot. Saka carries the psychological baggage from a penalty he missed in the final of the same tournament four years ago. Putting the benefits of practice aside, what Saka needs at this moment is psychological courage – and yes, he scored!

Successful past experiences can build confidence and help reduce imposter feelings. But, in Saka's case, his previous experience was negative. His missed penalty four years earlier contributed to his team's failure to win the tournament. As Saka said in an interview[1] after the 2024 match: 'You can fail once, but you have a choice whether you put yourself in that position again.'

It takes courage to put yourself in that position again.

It takes courage to learn from your failures and not let them define you.

It also takes courage to tackle your inner imposter feelings and accept how good you really are.

Courage

To simplify many hundreds of years of philosophical discussions, courage can be divided into three broad categories:

- *Physical courage* – acts performed by an individual despite the risk of death or physical harm,[2] such as saving someone from drowning.

- *Moral courage* – the willingness to act toward a moral or worthwhile goal, despite the presence of risk, uncertainty and fear,[3] such as standing up for what you believe to be right.

- *Psychological courage* – an inner courage to face irrational fears and anxieties,[4] such as overcoming an addiction.

While physical courage and moral courage are definitely needed in some situations, my hypothesis is that it is psychological courage that we need to help us overcome our imposter feelings. Up until now, research on psychological courage has focused on the courage needed to overcome negative situations, such as addictions or to escape from abusive relationships.[5]

However, I am interested in how psychological courage can be used in positive situations. While not explicitly mentioning psychological courage, psychology professor Paul Gilbert suggests that courage may be developed by replacing shame and self-criticism with compassion.[6] An example might be the courage needed to rethink your view of yourself to one that is more positive, to take on board the positive feedback you receive rather than dismiss it, or to accept how good you really are. This positive approach to psychological courage is rooted in the field of positive psychology, sometimes referred to as the 'Science of Happiness'. In my research, I define *positive psychological courage* as 'the courage to internalise our strengths, recognise the growth in knowledge, skills and abilities and to accept who we have grown into being'.[7] Positive psychological courage sounds rather academic and is a bit of a mouthful, so I often use the term inner courage when talking to people. The terms are interchangeable.

Looking at this from an academic perspective for a moment, the following diagram shows how the concepts in my research and this book fit together. In particular, how the field of positive psychology and positive psychological courage relate to the imposter phenomenon and coping strategies. In the diagram, positive psychology and psychological courage are in the bottom left and right corners of the triangle representing the foundations of my research in the field of psychology. The imposter phenomenon is in the middle, as it is the central focus of my research. By placing coping strategies pointing upwards at the top of the triangle, the aim is to illustrate the forward movement involved in coping and overcoming imposter feelings in the hope that we all continue to move forward, learn and develop, as no one truly stands still.

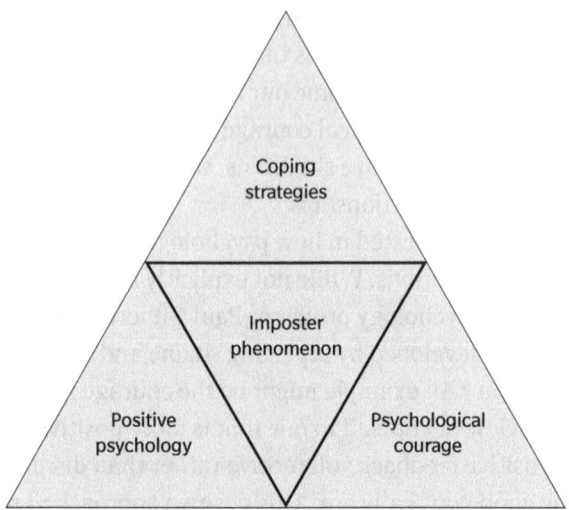

Relationship of positive psychology and positive psychological courage to the imposter phenomenon and coping strategies

During my research interviews, it became apparent from the comments made by my participants that they were learning about themselves as they shared their thoughts and experiences with me. Through discussing the concept of courage, my participants started to acknowledge that they had indeed been courageous, even when initially their thoughts were the opposite. Sometimes their acts of psychological courage were small and seemingly insignificant, such as turning a camera on in an online meeting, asking a question, or making an 'intervention' (in Cleo's words). But whether they were small actions or larger ones such as giving presentations, taking on a new role or asking for feedback, the actions were positive. The participants needed a degree of psychological courage to take these actions despite the imposter thinking going on inside their heads.

Discussing the concept of psychological courage and courageous acts helped my participants reflect on the topic:

Ben: 'I'm not aware that I've used courage. I've just, part of me is managing to do it. So I can't really use the word internal courage, but it obviously must be there and it is my internal courage that is winning in the situation.'

Fay: 'This is very much an internal thing, and that is about having the positive outcomes and holding yourself accountable to your own values and having the gumption to do that . . . courage is the strength to pull back to those values, to then say, "am I upholding them to myself?"'

Iris: 'I think it's making yourself a bit vulnerable by doing something that makes you feel uncomfortable.'

Quinn: 'Is it courage, or is it just . . . listening to it, understanding it and, I guess, just not necessarily going with those thoughts that are in your head? Acknowledging them and moving on.'

And as Pat's comment illustrates: 'Thinking about it in terms of internal courage is quite powerful.'

Time in

- What does positive psychological courage or inner courage mean to you?
- When have you used your inner (psychological) courage?

Rethink your self-view

As discussed in Chapter 4, some people tend to downplay their successes, dismiss their positive feedback and choose not to reflect on things that have gone well, as a way of staying humble.

How we see ourselves is often different from the way others perceive us. By taking time to reflect on the perceptions of others, and comparing with your self-perception, you will be able to spot the mismatches. In this extract from Holly's interview, she describes this mismatch when receiving feedback from her colleagues at a time she was moving jobs:

> **'When you move jobs, suddenly people come and see you or they send you unsolicited emails or send you cards and say: "Oh, I'm really sorry to see you go. You know, you're one of my favourite people. I really like working with you. I've learned so much from you. You are a real inspiration . . . blah, blah." And you go: "Well, that's really weird because it doesn't line up at all with the picture I have of myself".'**

By drawing on your inner courage, you will be able to rethink and update the view you have of yourself to one that is more accurate, that, ultimately, will be beneficial in reducing your imposter feelings. It may be uncomfortable to realise how good you really are, but, as Brené Brown[8] suggests:

> **'We can choose courage or we can choose comfort, but we can't have both.**
>
> **Not at the same time.'**

Another way of rethinking the view of yourself is what I call 'growing into yourself'. As our knowledge, skills and abilities grow over time, so should our perception of our knowledge, skills and abilities. But we often don't stop to take the time to update our self-view. Perhaps we need an inner voice that won't let us continue until we have updated our self-view – a little like software that forces an update upon us just as we are about to go into an online meeting. Frustrating as it may be, it may help our performance at work run more smoothly and with less stress if we were forced to be courageous and update our self-view from time to time.

An 'aha' moment

Several years ago, I was invited to speak on the imposter phenomenon at Oxford University's Women in Business student group. At the end of the talk, someone from the audience spoke to me about internalising the external feedback and providing evidence to help her overcome her imposter feelings. I can recall her saying: 'Surely, I know myself better than everyone else.' She was, of course, absolutely right, but I gently challenged her with the suggestion that she knows herself subjectively, whereas those who are providing her with feedback see her more objectively. I then asked: 'Which is the more accurate view?'

On the train home, I reflected on this discussion. I have also dismissed many positive feedback comments and been harsh in my judgement of myself, assuming that I knew myself better than anyone else. As I reflected, a thought occurred to me: perhaps it is arrogant to believe yourself above everyone else. I know that I have tended to dismiss positive feedback because I do not want to become arrogant. But maybe we are inadvertently doing the opposite and being arrogant by elevating our own subjective view of ourselves over and above the objective view of others.

Even if we do take time to reflect on the positive feedback and our achievements, we still tend not to update the view of ourselves. It is easier to hold on to your existing perception of yourself than to challenge yourself to think more positively about your knowledge, your skills and your capabilities. Accepting the positive comments from others won't make you arrogant, but dismissing them doesn't make you humble either! Instead, know what you are good at and what you are not so good at, and focus on the former.

Self-deception

Our view of ourselves can be very difficult to shift, whether to one that is more accurately positive or to one more accurately negative. We are very good at deceiving ourselves in order to keep our self-perception intact. Psychologists Daniel Putman[9] and Albert

Bandura[10] both describe negative examples of self-deception in their writing, such as someone not accepting their level of incompetence and avoiding learning from failures, ignoring criticism or discounting other negative evidence that does not align with their positive self-view.

However, the self-deception I'm talking about here involves ignoring positive evidence, and so not updating the self-view to a more positive one. There is a fear of owning one's greatness. It is counter to the childhood message of not getting too big for our boots. We don't want to appear arrogant or be seen as better than others (yet, secretly we may desire to be the best). We may also be worried that, if we accept how good we are, we then have our own perception to live up to, and what if we fall short?

As humans we also tend to look for evidence to confirm our original expectations (known as confirmation bias). This means we often have blind spots,[11] in this case failing to recognise what we have become good at or skilled in. Many is the time that I have had a conversation with someone who has chosen to ignore a positive outcome, or who has treated it as an exception, to maintain their negative view of their own ability, albeit subconsciously at times. And positive feedback, well, that can easily be discounted or deleted (especially if received by email). Bandura suggests that 'if the evidence is compellingly persuasive, however, most [people] eventually alter their self-beliefs'.[12] So if there is enough compelling positive evidence, we may eventually update our self-belief.

Having an opportunity to update your view of yourself can come from trigger events or extraordinary moments where your actions are brought into the limelight or when praise is received from others.[13] However, these events can be viewed as exceptional and may be overlooked or discounted if we don't make the effort to reflect on them and internalise them.[14] One way to avoid self-deception is to consciously create a 'self-portrait' that accurately reflects times when you have been at your best. This may help you take a more objective view and update your perception of yourself. I am not referring to an artistic self-portrait, but one consisting of examples, tasks you have completed, and situations you have encountered – a little like those Quinn mentioned in creating his positive playlist, or my confidence wall.

Both effort and courage are needed to update the self-view and avoid self-deception, which leads to the next section about remembering the good.

Remember the good

'Bad is stronger than good'[15] is the title of a much-quoted journal article in the field of positive psychology. The inference is that human evolution has given us the propensity to recall adverse events with a stronger emotional response than positive events. Bad feedback, failures, mistakes and, indeed, any negative experience, all have a more significant emotional impact and a longer-lasting impact than positive experiences. But we do receive positive feedback, we do have positive experiences, and we do achieve success – we just need to make an extra effort to remember them.

In the previous chapter, I encouraged you to practise a three-step technique to help you accept your positive feedback: keep it, review it and 'yes, and . . . ' it. To counteract the tendency to remember the negative (developmental) feedback, some researchers[16] suggest that it is helpful to focus on the details, differences and nuances of positive events, a process termed 'mindful organising'. You can try applying this approach to positive feedback: What specifically was being said? Where were you? What happened? What did you do? How do you feel about the outcome? This can help embed the memory more deeply, making it easier to recall at a later date.

If you are not getting as much positive feedback as you would like, or the feedback is very generalised, you could be courageous and ask for more feedback and ask for it to be specific. Some people feel uncomfortable and worry they will be perceived as 'needy' by asking for positive feedback. To avoid this, you could phrase the request along the lines of: 'Which part of the project do you think I did most successfully?' or 'What specifically do you mean by "a good job"?' or 'What do you think I did for the project to have worked out so well?' I recently took my own advice and asked a client what they meant when they thanked me for 'being easy to work with'. Their reply was surprising because it was such a simple action: replying promptly to emails. Not a very high bar to reach, but it clearly made a difference to them.

As mentioned in the previous chapter, by making a concerted effort to focus on your positive feedback, you will also raise your awareness of your strengths. This will help create a more positive view of yourself,[17] enabling you to update your self-view and reduce your imposter thoughts.

Sadly, it isn't that easy. If it was, there would be no need for this book. Some of my participants paused for a very long time when I asked them to reflect on a time when they had thought about themselves more positively after a success or after receiving positive feedback. Nina eventually responded: 'Oof! That's not easy, that's not easy, have I done that?' Pat exclaimed: 'Oh my goodness, I need a couch to lie down on for this!' Holly said that she had not rethought her self-view but had rethought the way others see her: 'I mean, maybe not rethinking but re-evaluating how others perceive me.'

While imposter thoughts may distort a person's self-view and lead to the dismissal of positive feedback, we can be encouraged by the fact that we all have the potential to view ourselves more objectively. Take some time to reflect on your achievements, past successes and your aims for the future.

Courage or confidence?

When facilitating workshops on developing confidence, I often find that what people are really talking about is a need for courage. Confidence grows through experience, success and positive outcomes. It is courage that helps us to take the first step towards gaining that experience.

Some of my research participants expressed confusion about which came first, courage or confidence, and whether acting courageously would help them overcome their imposter thoughts.

Fay could not decide whether her inner courage would exist without her imposter thoughts:

'I can't work out if they are acid and alkaline and they balance each other out, or whether they are fish and chips, you know, they go so well together. Courage is "yes, you can." But my courage wouldn't say "yes, you can" if my imposter wasn't saying "no, you can't".'

Iris describes how she uses courage to manage her imposter feelings:

'I feel like using your internal courage is a tool to manage those imposter feelings, in that it's thinking: "I feel that way, but I'm going to try and do this anyway." I think it's a tool to try and deal with them, to be brave. I do want to grow and develop and challenge myself and be the best I can be, and I don't think that's possible without sometimes being a bit vulnerable and just doing it.'

Gail saw the juxtaposition differently, as a battle between her courage and her imposter thoughts:

'They battle each other constantly, don't they? You've got your courageous side wanting to come forward and speak up in that meeting. You want to be the one to ask that question. You want to be the one to come up with a very valid point. But the imposter syndrome says to you, "this is a very important meeting, with people from America and they're big leaders. What if you ask the wrong question, what if it sounds stupid?" So that is constantly an internal battle.'

While research indicates that confidence grows over time and through new experiences,[18] for those with imposter thoughts that doesn't always happen. Iris illustrates this well when she says:

> 'I've been in the industry for just under eight years and most definitely experienced times of feeling a bit wobbly and unsure of myself because it was new, and I quite frequently experience those now.'

One of the most evocative descriptions of imposter thoughts I've heard, and how they can detract from a sense of confidence, came from Nina:

> 'It's a cycle, I think: "I know I can do this, and I'm good to do this" and, after a while, it's like, "what am I doing here?" and I go back and rethink it again and again. I think we're the worst critics of ourselves. I've had colleagues with the same kinds of thoughts and every time I've thought, "oh, come on, how are you gonna be worried, you're great, you're super good at what do you do, why are you doubting yourself?" And then it comes to your own mind: "Ok, I'm giving all this encouragement to these people but I'm not giving it to my myself. What's wrong with me?" It's like you're your own flagellation monster.'

Are your inner thoughts your own 'flagellation monster'? Developing psychological courage may help bring that monster into check. Recognising courageous acts helps to create a sense of courage. But how do you go about choosing to be courageous in the first place?

Roz Savage MBE has created a helpful mnemonic for choosing to develop courage.[19] Roz has rowed across three oceans single-handed, so she knows a lot about acting courageously:

C alling

O wnership

U ncertainty

R esources

A ction

G rit

E volve

First, Roz suggests that you need a strong reason to act, a *Calling*. So why do you want to speak up in that meeting? To challenge that decision? To pursue that promotion? The why compels you to leave your safe zone.

The next step is to take *Ownership*. I like the phrase, 'if it is to be, it is up to me.' You are the one who can make things happen. There is no need to wait for others to grant you permission.

If you do choose to act courageously, there is no certainty that everything will work out as you wanted. You'll need to be ok with a bit of *Uncertainty*.

But you can draw upon your *Resources*. These are the knowledge, skills and abilities that you have built up over time. Your resources also include your cheerleaders – your line manager, your colleagues, your friends and your family. Ask them for help or support when you need it.

Take *Action*. Just do it.

But if at first you don't succeed . . . then try, try and try again. A little *Grit* and determination can go a long way.

Finally, once you have done all of the above, you will have learnt something, gained a new skill, or increased your abilities. You will have *Evolved*. The key to developing courage, and reducing your imposter feelings, is to recognise that you are not the same person that you were when you set out at the start. I'd suggest it is time for a psychologically courageous update of your self-view to one that is more positive.

Time in

- Have you been engaging in self-deception to stay safe?
- What is your self-view? Have you updated it after reading this chapter?
- Who will support you in your quest for courage?
- What courageous step could you take first?
- What courageous step could you take next?

part 3

How managers and leaders can support others

chapter 9

How leaders and managers can help people with imposter feelings to flourish in the workplace

'The brave may not live forever, but the cautious do not live at all.'[1]

Richard Branson

There are some people fortunate enough not to experience imposter feelings. If you have never felt like an imposter, it can be hard to understand what it feels like and why some excellent team players don't like praise, won't speak up in meetings, or turn down promotions. I have even had managers tell me that they have lost very capable team members through poor performance that they now believe might have been down to imposter feelings holding the person back from contributing effectively at work.

Organisations may also miss out if individuals who feel like imposters don't feel safe speaking up. Ideas may not be shared, assumptions may not be challenged, and decisions may not be thoroughly debated before being made. In Chapter 2, I looked at the research into the impact of imposter feelings on individuals. The impact on organisations is less well-researched.

Hopefully, as a manager or leader, you want the best *for* your team, not just the best *from* your team. You want to support them, help develop their talents, help them progress in their careers and flourish at work. This chapter contains ways you can support colleagues and team members who you suspect, or even know, are experiencing imposter feelings. You don't have to be a leader or a manager to support others; the ideas suggested here may apply equally well with colleagues and perhaps even with family members.

Awards, accolades, praise, promotion and positive feedback are all well-intentioned ways of acknowledging how well someone is doing in their job. However, despite the individual's desire to succeed, success can be very hard to internalise,[2] especially for someone experiencing imposter feelings. So these ways of recognising how well someone is performing may not be as effective as you think.

How can I spot the imposter phenomenon in others?

When someone experiences the imposter phenomenon, they are feeling like a fraud on the inside *despite the external evidence of success*. This can make spotting imposter feelings in others difficult, especially if you are more senior, as showing any sign of weakness to you may be an absolute no-no for those your junior. What you see at work will most likely be someone who is very competent, confident and capable. But there are some clues you can look for that may indicate imposter feelings lie beneath the surface. Note I said indicate; remember not to diagnose or label people with the imposter phenomenon.

One clue to look for is unnecessary overwork. Perhaps the employee works late in the evening, sends emails outside of working hours, or researches and provides lots more information than is really necessary. This can indicate a desire for perfection, which, as already discussed, is associated with imposter feelings. It is essential to distinguish unnecessary overwork from extra work. Of course, there are times in most jobs when working additional hours just has to be done, for instance, to meet a deadline.

Confusingly, procrastination can also be an indicator of the imposter phenomenon. Researchers[3] found that individuals experiencing the imposter phenomenon tend to procrastinate, especially if their work is not yet 'perfected' to their own high standards. So not getting work in on time and missing deadlines are also clues that imposter feelings might be present. They might fob you off by saying, 'it isn't done yet' or be hesitant to tell you where they are up to, or unwilling to share early drafts. This can easily be misinterpreted as laziness, leading to poor performance reviews despite the employee actually being capable of performing to the required standard.

Another clue to consider is how individuals react to positive feedback. Most of us have learnt that we should say 'thank you' when we receive positive feedback, but that does not mean the feedback has been internalised. A polite verbal 'thank you' does not constitute acceptance of the feedback. A quick shrug of the shoulders, a slight eye roll, a fleeting grimace, or perhaps a glance away are subtle clues that the feedback may have been dismissed. Other not-so-subtle cues that positive feedback is being rejected are verbal responses such as 'I'm just doing my job', 'anyone could have done it', 'it was nothing really' or 'it wasn't me, it was the team'. While these signs do not guarantee that the person is feeling like an imposter, they are indications that imposter feelings may be lurking beneath the surface.

More straightforwardly, you may also find yourself in the privileged position where a team member comes to you and tells you that they are 'suffering from the imposter syndrome'. This is the language I generally hear people use, although, as explained in the early chapters, I prefer to use 'experiencing' and 'phenomenon'. In these situations, you are in no doubt about their feelings but it is still important not to make assumptions or to try to 'fix' them.

How to support others

If you think you have spotted imposter feelings through one of the clues above or another behaviour that indicates your colleague or team member is not recognising their knowledge, skills and abilities at work, then gently call it out. But, please, not by pointedly saying, 'aha, that's your imposter talking!' I suggest you start by asking questions, being curious as to how they are feeling and what they are thinking, rather than providing a label yourself.

You could start by asking:

- I notice that you are sending emails late at night. It's important to take some downtime away from work. How are you managing to do that?

- You seem reluctant to share a draft of your work. Is there a reason for that? How can I help you feel more comfortable sharing early drafts?

- When I gave you that feedback just now, I noticed that you looked a bit uncomfortable. What were you thinking as I spoke?

> *If someone tells you they feel like an imposter, you could ask:*
>
> - Could you help me understand how that feels?
> - Where do you think those feelings come from?
> - What evidence do you have that supports them (those feelings)?
> - What evidence do you have that contradicts them (those feelings)?
>
> *Then perhaps also ask:*
>
> - What makes the feeling worse/better?
>
> *These questions are useful for coaches as well as for managers who wish to put themselves into a coaching role to have a conversation with their colleague or team member.*

Asking a few probing questions, with kindness, around their thinking and encouraging the person to find evidence both for and against the thoughts can be a relief for the individual. They no longer have to 'pretend' to you that they are capable. If appropriate, it might be helpful to share with them times that you have personally experienced imposter thoughts. Research indicates that discussing imposter thoughts and having a supportive manager really does help reduce imposter feelings.[4]

Don't tell people they are amazing

While intending to be supportive, positive comments can sometimes make imposter feelings even worse.[5] I experienced this early on in my PhD studies. One wet winter morning, I cycled the 15-minute ride from home to the university campus for a training session on academic writing, only to be horrified to find that I was an hour late. I had put the wrong time into my calendar and the training session was in full flow as I entered the room. What made it even worse was that my supervisor was leading it. Now she really will know how incompetent I am!

I sheepishly took my seat, and in the break went to apologise for being late. My supervisor's response was, 'oh, I've got no worries about you.' But, instead of her positive comment making me feel better, her words had precisely the opposite effect. I didn't believe her; my instant reaction was, 'but I have worries about me.' The impact of her words just widened the gap in my mind between how well I was perceived externally and how close I felt to failing internally.

This small example indicates how easily positive comments can have unintended negative consequences, increasing imposter feelings rather than alleviating them. If the recipient is experiencing the imposter phenomenon, providing praise or generalised feedback is often not received as supportive. Instead of feeling warm and fuzzy on the inside when told how amazing they are, the recipient may feel pressurised, and their mind may be saying:

- Oh yikes, now I've got to live up to your expectations!
- Ok, but I bet you say that to everyone.
- Hmm, what do you want now?
- It wasn't that good a job.
- I could have done it better if I'd had more time.
- Thanks, but anyone could have done it, and probably better.

Thus, the positive feedback is dismissed: deleted, distorted or generalised.

What is helpful is detailed and specific feedback rather than general, subjective reassurance. Now, I realise that leading a team means you are often time-poor and can't spend a long time with each person. But a few extra seconds could make all the difference. Don't tell people they are amazing; instead, tell them *why* they are amazing. If my supervisor had told me why she had no worries about me, I might have received her comment in a totally different way. I had no one to compare myself with or even a past experience to reference myself against. On the other hand, my supervisor had supervised many students over the years and could have given me a quick insight into her perspective of how I was really doing.

Receiving generalised positive feedback was also an issue for Cleo and Nina, as these extracts illustrate:

Cleo: 'I've got good feedback; the level below the minister actually said: "Oh, Cleo made a really good point," and I also got praised afterwards by my line manager: "That was a great intervention." It didn't change my view of myself. I just felt like they were just trying to be nice and they have overly exaggerated how good that intervention was.'

Nina: 'If someone is telling you you're so good, then sometimes, it's also a lack of trust in people. They tell you: "Oh, you're so good" and you're like: "Are you telling me that because it's true or because you want something from me?"'

The hardest part is remembering to be specific in your praise. Don't over-inflate your praise by using words such as amazing, incredible, awesome or even great.[6] Don't generalise your praise either.

When I was a member of Toastmasters,[7] a public speaking organisation, we were encouraged to use the word 'critique' when giving feedback on one another's speeches. This meant the feedback contained what was good about the speech as well as what could be improved. There is also the structure of using What Went Well, Even Better If (WWW EBI) when giving feedback. This is used in some schools and workplaces and the structure encourages feedback to contain something good as well as a point for improvement. So when giving feedback to ourselves or others, I suggest that you recognise and acknowledge What Went Well and, if necessary, point out what could be Even Better If.

While WWW EBI seems a good structure for giving feedback, I am worried that using this structure for feedback all the time may, in fact, increase imposter feelings. A feedback technique that involves always saying how something could be improved means the outcome is never good enough (in imposter-style thinking). This can exacerbate perfectionistic tendencies, which, if you had a hypercritical parent, you are likely to recognise what I am talking about. Try giving just What Went Well, Full Stop feedback and resist the temptation to suggest improvements; even if there could be some improvements, do they really matter? Sometimes, we simply need to know that what has been done is good enough and that good enough is just that: good enough.

➤ Mix up your feedback when giving it to others and use What Went Well, Full Stop (WWW.) feedback as well as WWW EBI (What Went Well, Even Better If)

Use strengths in your feedback

When preparing to give positive feedback to someone, take a moment to think about that person's strengths. Then name the strength and weave the word 'strength' into your feedback. For example: 'Thanks for the effort you put in to make that project a success. I noticed in particular that you (. . . kept the customer up to speed throughout), and I see (. . . your ability to create a good rapport) as one of your strengths.'

I believe the use of the word 'strength' in the feedback helps to bypass what I call the *imposter filter*, which filters out and ignores information that does not match the person's self-perception and is very adept at dismissing positive feedback. But, if the feedback is specific, strengths-based and names the strength, it is more likely to bypass the imposter filter and be internalised.

➤ Remember to not only name a strength in the feedback, but also use the word 'strength' when giving feedback.

Make useful comparisons in your feedback

Making comparisons can help the receiver understand where the bar is. No, not the one that serves drinks, but the standard we need to attain. Those experiencing imposter feelings often set their bar far higher than necessary and spend many hours over-preparing, potentially heading towards burnout. Providing specific comparisons when giving feedback to frame the positive message can help prevent the other person's imposter chatter from making unhelpful or untrue comparisons.

Recently, I presented a session on 'Leading with Courage' at a conference in London. I received some lovely feedback from my client along the lines of, 'that was amazing', which was very gratifying. However, it was some unsolicited feedback from the event's audio-visual technician that really landed for me. Rather than telling me that my session was amazing, he was very specific about what he thought I did well. Because of his experience of watching many professional speakers, he was able to make an objective comparison with other conference speakers. He told me that I brought authenticity to the topic, that I was flexible when taking questions and that I did not pretend to have all the answers. This very specific feedback was difficult for my imposter chatter to contradict; I was very grateful to the technician for taking the time to pass on his observations. Rightly or wrongly, I was more inclined to believe his feedback than my client's – my imposter chatter was saying that the client might just have been being polite while the technician did not need to say anything at all to me.

> What comparisons could you include to make the feedback you give to others more impactful?

Provide positive feedback in a way that will be received positively

There used to be an adage when I worked in banking of 'praise in public, reprimand in private'. However, given the comments from some of my participants, this may be too generalised. Not everyone likes receiving praise. For example, you may recall that when she receives praise, Nina said: 'I feel like I have to just go under the table' and Ellie declared she finds it 'quite embarrassing to get good feedback'. Roger told me: 'I can't think of a time where I've accepted it [positive feedback] and actually felt proud about it, or taken it on board without being negative about it.' Kelly was concerned about being judged negatively by others, explaining why she doesn't take on board positive feedback: 'I wouldn't want to be seen as being big-headed.'

When providing positive feedback to a member of your team, take some time to consider not just the content but also who is receiving it. What do you think their preference would be? Public or private? Also, think about how you will deliver it. Sending it by email might appear to be a good solution, but people have told me that if they receive a positive email, they delete it – and I mean completely delete it, not just put it in the deleted items folder.

> Giving positive feedback in person, followed up by a short email, and repeating your message might be more effective.

Repetition

When giving positive feedback, you can be forgiven for thinking that you've done your job once the feedback has been delivered. As I'm sure you are now realising, simply giving positive feedback to those experiencing imposter feelings is not enough to ensure it is received, heard and taken on board. Giving positive feedback more frequently might help. A suggestion made by researchers Marilyn Whitman and Kristen Shanine[8] was that providing support through regular, informal feedback may help reduce imposter feelings in team members. The two key aspects to highlight here are: regular and informal. Maybe you could add a regular diary reminder to do this more often, but be careful not to make it contrived – you don't want to inadvertently create a 'Terrific Tuesday' or 'Thankful Thursday'.

Quinn highlighted the importance of hearing positive messages more than once from someone whose opinion he trusted and also how regular personal development talks have also helped him to believe in himself more:

'I think it's probably two things. One is the integrity of the person giving the review. Someone who I trust and someone who I know will give the bad news or the negative feedback. The second bit is the cumulative impact of the last year and a half of talks on mental health, well-being, and understanding how the brain works. I'm now at the point where, perhaps the second time around or third time around I hear this, I can do something with it. I perhaps discounted it beforehand.'

Since formal evaluations such as performance appraisals can heighten imposter feelings, drip-feeding positive feedback in a less threatening format may be beneficial. There is no precise formula for the frequency, but research in positive psychology indicates that positive feedback needs to be given more frequently than negative feedback to maintain a balance of positivity.[9]

➤ How regularly do you give positive feedback to your team members?

One-to-ones and performance appraisals

As we have seen, formal feedback through one-to-ones and performance reviews can be stressful, particularly for those experiencing the imposter phenomenon. While you may not be able to change the organisation's procedures, as a manager you can be mindful of the stress these meetings can cause and the tendency of those with imposter thoughts to downplay their successes or even generate negative self-evaluations.[10]

My own experiences of performance reviews goes back to the 1990s. At Barclays Bank, we had what was known as the 'green sheet' to complete before our annual performance reviews. On the green A4 form (yes, the clue was in the name), we were expected to evaluate our own performance and state how well we had done over the past 12 months. We also had to write about our career aspirations and where we wanted to be in five years' time. I remember dreading writing on it, not knowing how to assess myself or how to phrase successes. Were they really successes? What had I actually achieved? As for career aspirations, I recall thinking, 'I don't know where I want to be in five years' time . . . but I probably won't be working here.' I wasn't going to write that on the sheet!

Being observed, assessed, supervised or examined can trigger imposter thoughts, as in this example from Lisa: 'What's odd is I do feel confident about my abilities in my job when I'm in my job and doing it. It is when anyone else starts looking at what I'm doing or asking a question that I feel less confident about what I'm doing. Crazy!' Una's experience of the imposter phenomenon was exacerbated every time she met with her manager: 'It's back to feeling like I'm gonna be found out. What's she got for me today?'

Organisations also need to be aware of how well their managers conduct appraisals. Fay found herself another job after a poor appraisal. But Fay hadn't performed poorly; she unfortunately had a manager who handled appraisals badly: 'One bad appraisal, where my manager gave the same appraisal to all of his direct reports – he learned the script, he gave the same thing – it was unbelievable. It knocked my confidence completely. What is the biggest impact his comments had on me? I left.'

If handled well, appraisals and one-to-ones can be very supportive. Quinn highlighted the benefits he gained from an effective annual review: 'My recent annual review with my manager actually put me in a really good mood and helped change my perspective on where I was at with things. I've struggled with certain bits, but there's a lot of good things that I do, and she really emphasised the positives.'

The tendency of imposter thoughts to generate negative self-evaluations can be counteracted by encouraging self-comparisons to identify areas of growth. Another technique is to make discussions achievement-focused, highlighting successful tasks, projects or presentations. As already mentioned, giving strengths-based feedback during regular meetings, such as one-to-ones and performance appraisals, can work well too.

➤ How will you help others objectively evaluate their performance?

External recognition

Those with imposter feelings may be inclined to filter out praise if it comes from their manager or anyone who is perceived as potentially having an ulterior motive. The imposter filter may find excuses to discount praise, internally saying: 'You're just saying that because you want something from me . . . ' Recognition may seem more credible if it comes from an external source.[11] Kelly spoke about receiving recognition from outside the organisation and its benefit in reducing her imposter thoughts. Positive comments from her manager had made no difference, but feedback she received from two strangers did:

'The fact that everybody internally will say I'm doing the right thing [which is dismissed] and then two strangers can say something, and I think "Oh, yeah, I'm maybe doing the right thing".'

As we saw in Chapter 6, external recognition also helped create a more positive self-perception for Iris. Her nomination for an industry award served 'an organisational reputational purpose, in that it's good for organisational profile and I can totally get the strategy behind it. So, it's not all about me. But, at the same time, it's really helped me; it does indicate some recognition of what I have been contributing recently.'

More research is needed to determine whether external recognition, through formal or informal awards, could be another way to reduce imposter thoughts. Anecdotally, providing objective external recognition certainly seems to help.

➤ What awards, internally or industry-wide, can you nominate your staff for?

Facilitate learning from mistakes

In Chapter 7, I discussed the benefits of reframing failures into learning opportunities. When mistakes happen while you are in charge, it can be tempting to be harsh on the individuals involved. However, if the errors are genuine, a different approach may benefit the individual, the team and the organisation.

One of my clients had a development team that made a massive mistake when launching a new product. It resulted in a significant financial loss for the organisation; the product had to be withdrawn and reworked before it could be returned to market. Instead of launching an investigation there and then, the development team left the mistake alone for six months. When I met them, they had just reviewed the product launch. They told me that the emotions were too raw in the early days after making the mistake, and it would not have been reviewed objectively. But review it they did – having waited for what the team felt was an appropriate length of time to provide the ability to separate the emotional reaction from what actually happened. Lessons learned were sought, and new processes were devised to prevent it from happening again.

The organisation's positive, learning-based approach to this mistake made the team feel valued, although I don't know how they felt as individuals or whether their imposter feelings were impacted. Research indicates that, if a climate of fear and judgement prevails, imposter feelings are likely to persist, and the potential for hiding mistakes, rather than learning from them, increases.[12]

Many organisations launch immediate reviews into mistakes, which may be appropriate depending on the nature of the error and the nature of the organisation. However, if small mistakes are discussed openly, there is a chance that other more significant mistakes may be prevented. Taking a learning-based approach, discussing regularly what happened, how people felt and what was learnt – maybe even as a standing item on team meeting agendas – could create a climate of learning rather than one of hiding mistakes. This is done effectively in the aviation industry, which has worked to change its culture from mistakes and blame to one of learning.[13]

➤ How are mistakes viewed in your team or organisation? Where might you have more learning conversations?

Set clear expectations

Setting an expectation of what 'good' looks like can help manage overwork, reduce pressure and alleviate imposter feelings. When I was on Barclays Bank's training team, our appraisal system was revamped from the green sheet mentioned earlier to one that included a set of standards explicitly outlining what good looked like (as well as poor and excellent). Each appraisal was discussed in detail against the standards, with evidence provided by the appraisee and the line manager and reviewed against each goal. While it was onerous as the record-keeping was all on paper in those days, it was rigorous and transparent.

Providing clear expectations means there is no need to second-guess the standards or apply standards that are higher than necessary. As a manager, you may be required to set expectations, agree on performance levels and behaviours, and set goals. These are often co-created, so if you listen carefully to the suggestions of your team members, you might hear some of their hesitancy or high expectations, giving clues to the imposter thoughts beneath the surface. By agreeing in detail on the quality and quantity of what is expected, those you work with will have a clear understanding of the optimal standard.

➤ What does 'good' look like in your team, and is everyone aware of the standard?

Encourage contributions

As discussed in Chapter 5, organisations and teams may miss out on alternative ideas and be at risk of groupthink because individuals with imposter feelings feel uncomfortable speaking up, particularly in meetings. To counter this you need a non-judgmental meeting environment that encourages contributions from everyone and is open to challenge and discussion – easier said than done, I know.

This is where actions speak louder than words. Looking back again to my banking days, I remember a time when my office was on the ground floor but most of the other managers had offices on the third floor. One Friday morning as I climbed the stairs to the weekly managers meeting, a new series of posters had been printed and placed up the staircase. The posters declared, 'you are now entering a no-blame zone'. How odd, I thought. Was this a blame zone yesterday? What's changed? Of course, absolutely nothing had changed, other than the posters.

If you genuinely want to have contributions in meetings from everyone, you will need to invite them to speak. Asking 'has anyone got anything to add?' will probably be met with silence from anyone with imposter feelings. Some people may prefer to be primed before the meeting. That way, they know you will be asking for their ideas; otherwise, they may feel you are putting them on the spot. You could encourage contributions by inviting people to speak by using their name, which recognises you haven't heard from them. Verbally acknowledge their knowledge in the area being discussed and ask them to comment. This can reassure those whose imposter feelings are telling them that they shouldn't be there and that they don't have the right to speak up. You could also give people the space and time in a meeting to talk to the person next to them – maybe by leaving the room for five minutes, then they won't be inhibited by your presence. You will also need to manage judgements from others in meetings as too many voices are shut down with a comment of 'that won't work' or 'we've tried that already'.

> How frequently do people contribute in your meetings? Do you get to hear from everyone? If not, how could you encourage the quieter members to contribute?

Creating a culture that accepts that mistakes and failures will happen, is compassionate, and seeks to learn from mistakes takes time and effort. If you have the right intention, you can make a difference to people experiencing the imposter phenomenon. By supporting them, the whole team will benefit as well as, hopefully, the organisation.

Time in

- -

- When and how do you give positive feedback to your team members?
- Are performance appraisals a two-way conversation or more of a one-way exercise?
- When do you use strengths-based feedback?
- How could you provide recognition for the work your team do?
- What type of learning environment are you creating with your team?
- Are your team members willing to discuss their mistakes with you?
- Are your expectations clear to everyone in your team?
- How could you encourage more contributions, especially in meetings?

- -

Training, coaching and mentoring

Some researchers[14] have suggested that offering small-group training on the imposter phenomenon may help reduce imposter feelings. Suggestions for the content of these sessions include altering how failures and successes are perceived and internalised, understanding and normalising the imposter phenomenon, and following up with one-to-one coaching sessions. This type of intervention has not yet been rigorously researched, but anecdotal evidence supports the benefit of speaking to others about imposter experiences in helping people feel connected and less alone. Workshops or facilitated conversations may also help individuals reflect on their inner thoughts, and working in groups can help people rethink their self-perception.[15] But I recommend an element of caution in how you suggest a workshop to a member of your team. Telling them they should attend because you think they have 'imposter syndrome' might not go down too well. Perhaps framing it by saying that you can see how good they are, but you don't think they see it themselves and that the workshop might help, would be received more positively. (Or you could leave a copy of this book lying around!)

There is evidence that individual coaching may help individuals be more reflexive[16] enabling them to examine their feelings, motives and reactions more objectively by discussing them with someone else. If you are coaching someone, whether in a formal or informal capacity, and they tell you that they feel like an imposter, I suggest you ask a few questions to help them understand where this feeling may come from. It is likely to be helpful to do this before you guide them through strategies to overcome the imposter phenomenon.

The questions I favour are along the following lines – word them appropriately for the individual, your style and the situation:

- What specifically are you thinking or feeling?
- How is that affecting you?
- What is it that makes you think/feel like that?
- Where do you think it might come from?
- What evidence do you have that supports your thoughts/feelings?
- What evidence do you have that contradicts your thoughts/feelings?

I think it is important to ask the last two questions in that order. As mentioned earlier, human beings are prone to confirmation bias, leading individuals to favour information which aligns with their current beliefs, rather than immediately challenge those beliefs.[17] As you know by now, telling someone how good they are won't cut through their imposter chatter. Even if you tell them their strengths, they may not believe you because they might not feel heard. So begin by exploring their thoughts and feelings and encourage them to find evidence for and then against their feelings. Then, if appropriate, you can provide some specific evidence that contradicts their imposter thoughts.

> The following comments from participants in some of my workshops highlight the benefits of workshops and facilitated conversations about the imposter phenomenon. Of course, as a keynote speaker, trainer and workshop facilitator, I must admit to being biased on this point!

'I now recognise that my own perfectionism at work is, in part, a response to my imposter feelings and it has been a relief to adopt a more pragmatic approach as a result! Recognising that this phenomenon may affect colleagues, irrespective of how confident they may appear, is also helping me as an HR professional when seeking to support, encourage and empower colleagues.'

'I found it a bit confronting at times (a good thing), ticking off the things about myself (not able to take compliments easily, etc.) so I continue to be a work in progress. You gave me hope that I just need to keep on working on myself and it's worth it!'

'It was really helpful to reflect on these issues and come away with tools to get started with. I also wanted to say that your kind and open approach to facilitating group discussions was really helpful and I think this made us all feel very comfortable.'

'Personally, it has given me some hope that I can change, or at least improve. I can also look at my history and think of how much I have achieved rather than looking at the things I haven't done or haven't done well. It has also enabled me to see other people's struggles and issues.'

'Being able to get through some working days with less anxiety and stress will reduce the feeling of exhaustion at evenings and weekends.'

'The skills we've discussed regarding how to change our thinking and recognise that even if we aren't successful in doing something, it doesn't mean we did anything wrong, but that something has gone wrong along the way, and that might be systems-based.'

'I would love to join in one of your sessions again; it was life changing!'

But don't take my word for it or those of previous workshop participants; try it out for yourself. After reading this book, you now understand more about the imposter phenomenon. You could begin raising awareness of it by having conversations in team meetings or on away days.

Listen carefully to the feedback – people may initially feel awkward, but that does not mean the conversations aren't beneficial. Focus on strengths and successes, reframe failures as learning opportunities and be specific in your feedback to others. This will help you to create a supportive, compassionate workplace environment.

Be heart-led rather than head-led. You will find that the rewards follow.

Remember the importance of kindness

Given all that is happening in the world, we may need to be reminded to be kind to each other and to ourselves. Even though 13 November is World Kindness Day,[18] we can show kindness every day through our actions; it is something we embody. Taking the time to listen to another person talk about their imposter experiences is an act of kindness. Don't try to fix them; they don't need fixing or telling how wonderful they are. Remember to be kind to yourself too.

A note for HR

Those who work in organisational functions such as human resources (HR), talent management or employee well-being are often aware of the term imposter syndrome and may be seeking a solution to the 'problem'. If you have read the rest of the book before reaching this section, you will know by now that the term syndrome pathologises the experience of feeling like a fraud and is technically incorrect. Phenomenon, being an occurrence at specific points in time, or in certain situations, is a more accurate term. And that while individuals experience these imposter feelings, the organisational environment or the corporate culture can exacerbate them. For some people, feeling like an imposter or a fraud creates intense feelings of anxiety, potentially resulting in mental-health difficulties. However, in and of itself, the imposter phenomenon is not a mental-health condition.

So why reiterate this here?

HR departments are often tasked with creating policies and procedures to protect staff, focusing on well-being and health and safety, among other areas. Personally, I don't think there is a need for an 'imposter syndrome' policy. However, it would be beneficial for all human resources staff and people professionals to be aware of the imposter thinking that some employees may engage in. This can give an insight into the stress and anxiety that annual reviews, performance appraisals or career conversations can have for people with imposter-style thinking.

In 2021 the new ISO standard on Psychological Health and Safety at Work was published, ISO45003.[19] This standard is concerned with risks to mental health and well-being that can arise from the work environment. In some countries, such as Australia, the principles of the standard have been enshrined in law. ISO45003 provides a framework to inform good practice through which issues can be addressed, such as lack of role clarity, high job demands and the impact of planned changes – to cite just three examples of many. If an organisation is working towards ISO45003 certification, aware-ness of the imposter phenomenon could be incorporated into the policy framework. This may help HR professionals and managers provide a supportive environment and help alleviate imposter feel-ings. This could, in turn, aid a sense of belonging, increase positivity and, ultimately, productivity at work.

chapter 10

Conclusion

'It took me a long time to realise that I had made a reputation and I deserve it. Not probably or maybe. I deserve it.'

Kelly, *research participant*

Whether you are a manager or leader seeking to support someone in your team or are reading this book for yourself, thank you for reading it. I hope that you have picked up some useful information and actions. But please don't let the learning stop as you reach the end of the book. May I encourage you to have further conversations about the imposter phenomenon.

During my talks and workshops, I am often told how our discussions helped participants to develop new perspectives about themselves. This was also the case for the participants in my PhD research, to whom I will be forever grateful. As Simeon said:

'Just having a conversation about this with somebody who's willing to delve into strange places. It's quite helpful just to think these things through. I don't have many introspective conversations about this topic.'

Would it be beneficial to take this book to work and discuss it with your colleagues? Or could you take it to a book club and hold discussions there?

What are your actions?

As with any training course or speech, I hope you have enjoyed our 'conversations' throughout the book. But the key lies in the actions you take afterwards. Here are a few suggestions for you to 'stop' or 'start'.

- Stop telling other people they are amazing.
- Stop self-deprecating.
- Stop comparing yourself to others.
- Stop trying to be perfect.
- Stop holding on to an outdated view of yourself.

- Start collecting positive feedback, review it, and 'yes and . . .' it.
- Start giving objective, specific, strengths-based feedback.
- Start comparing yourself to yourself.
- Start recognising your courageous actions.
- Start reframing mistakes to learning opportunities.
- Start updating your self-view.

Time in

- How do you feel now after reading more about what the imposter phenomenon is and isn't?
- If you compare yourself to yourself, what have you learnt in the last 12 months?
- What skills have you developed? What experiences have you gained?
- What lessons have you learnt from failures?
- Where can you fail more and learn to be ok with that?
- When and where have you been courageous?
- How will you use psychological courage in the future?
- Are you prepared to feel uncomfortable and update your self-view to a more positive one?

And

- If you manage a team, what will you now do differently?

Appendix 1

How people cope in the workplace

How do people cope in the workplace when they experience imposter feelings? The table below indicates what makes imposter feelings worse and what helps to mitigate or lessen feelings of imposterism. You might have employed some of the following examples as a coping strategy for yourself. There is no one-size-fits-all, but these were the common themes from the interviews I conducted with 21 participants, all of whom reported experiencing frequent or intense imposter feelings.

Themes	Things that helped	Things that made it worse
External support	Managerial support	Lack of managerial support
	Colleagues' support	Poor leadership
	Corporate culture of humility and trust	Corporate culture of judgement
	Cheerleaders	Frequent changes in procedures
	Role models	Distorting positive feedback

➤

Themes	Things that helped	Things that made it worse
Belonging and otherness	Knowledge of the imposter phenomenon Having lots of skills and qualifications A sense of belonging	Qualifications, either having none or holding the 'wrong' qualification Gender stereotypes and societal expectations Lack of role models Meetings
Donning armour	Preparation & knowledge (often referred to as armour) Aiming for perfection Caveating suggestions Worst-case scenario planning Comparing self to others (to find where the 'bar' really is) Resilience Positive self-talk Reflection	Making mistakes Negative self-talk
Finding courage	Describing courage Thinking about how courage and imposter feelings interact 'Just have to' Updating self-view Interview lightbulbs	

Appendix 2

Coping strategies

Here is a list of the coping strategies covered in Chapter 7.

Knowing about the imposter phenomenon

Talk about it

You're not alone

Personify it

Don't fake it until you make it

Stop comparing yourself to others

    Start comparing yourself to yourself

    Remove your ego

An alternative comparison

Try working to 80 per cent

Don't do your best

Build your resilience

Practise self-compassion

Watch your self-talk

Give your confidence a boost

Find external evidence

Step one: Keep your positive feedback

Step two: Regularly review your positive feedback

Step three: 'Yes, and . . . ' your positive feedback

Know and own your strengths

Reframe failure

Practise failing safely

Rewrite your story

Appendix 3

___

Recommended reading

There are so many books I could recommend . . . this is a summary of those I have referenced in this book, plus a few more that I have on my shelves that I have found useful and thought-provoking (and a couple I have written!).

Arbinger Institute (2008) *Leadership and Self-deception: Getting Out of the Box*. ReadHowYouWant. com.

Atkin, K. (2015) *The Confident Manager: Lessons in Confidence and Communication for Successful Managers*. SRA Books.

Atkin, K. (2015) *The Presentation Workout: The 10 Tried-And-Tested Steps That Will Build Your Presenting And Pitching*. Pearson UK.

Ben-Shahar, T. (2009) *Pursuit of Perfect*. McGraw Hill Professional.

Brown, B. (2022) *The Gifts of Imperfection: Let Go of Who You Think You're Supposed to Be and Embrace Who You Are*. Simon and Schuster (tenth anniversary edition).

Cain, S. (2013) *Quiet: The Power of Introverts in a World That Can't Stop Talking*. Crown.

Carson, R. D. (1983) *Taming Your Gremlin: A Guide to Enjoying Yourself*. Perennial Library.

Clance, P. R. (1985) *The Impostor Phenomenon: Overcoming the Fear That Haunts Your Success*. Atlanta: Peachtree Publishing Ltd.

Cokley, K. (ed.) (2024) *The Impostor Phenomenon: Psychological Research, Theory, and Interventions*. American Psychological Association (this is academic and a very good summary of the research to date).

Cuddy, A. (2015) *Presence: Bringing Your Boldest Self to Your Biggest Challenges*. Hachette UK.

Curran, T. (2023) *The Perfection Trap: The Power of Good Enough in a World That Always Wants More*. Random House.

Duckworth, A. (2016) *Grit: The Power of Passion and Perseverance*. (Vol. 234). New York, NY: Scribner.

Dweck, C. (2017) *Mindset – Updated Edition: Changing the Way you Think to Fulfil your Potential*. Hachette UK.

Edmondson, A. (2018) *The Fearless Organization: Creating Psychological Safety in the Workplace for Learning, Innovation, and Growth*. New Jersey: John Wiley & Sons.

Johnstone, K. (2012) *Impro: Improvisation and the Theatre*. Routledge.

Kase, L. (2008) *The Confident Leader: How the Most Successful People Go from Effective to Exceptional*. McGraw Hill Professional.

Mackesy, C. (2022) *The Boy, the Mole, the Fox and the Horse: The Animated Story*. Random House.

Martin, S. (2007) *Born standing Up: A Comic's Life*. Simon and Schuster.

Perry, P. (2019) *The Book You Wish Your Parents Had Read (and Your Children Will Be Glad That You Did)* Penguin UK.

Reivich, K. and Shatté, A. (2002) *The Resilience Factor: 7 Essential Skills for Overcoming Life's Inevitable Obstacles*. Broadway books.

Appendix 4

Notes

Introduction

1   Villwock, J. A., Sobin, L. B., Koester, L. A. and Harris, T. M. (2016) Impostor syndrome and burnout among American medical students: A pilot study. *International Journal of Medical Education*, 7, p. 364.

2   Ben-Shahar, T. (2009) *The Pursuit of Perfect*. New York: McGraw Hill.

3   Clance, P. R. and Imes, S. A. (1978) The imposter phenomenon in high achieving women: Dynamics and therapeutic intervention. *Psychotherapy: Theory, Research & Practice*, 15(3), pp. 241–7.

4   Jones. R. (2015) What CEOs are afraid of. *Havard Business Review*. Available at: https://hbr.org/2015/02/what-ceos-are-afraid-of.

5   Atkin, K. (2024) How do individuals cope at work in the context of the Imposter Phenomenon? A thematic analysis study. Anglia Ruskin Research Online (ARRO). Thesis. Available at: https://doi.org/10.25411/aru.27325224.v1.

6   Clance, P. R. (1985) *The Impostor Phenomenon: Overcoming The Fear That Haunts Your Success.* Atlanta: Peachtree Pub. Ltd.

Chapter 1

1   Clance, P. R. and Imes, S. A. (1978) The imposter phenomenon in high achieving women: Dynamics and therapeutic intervention. *Psychotherapy: Theory, Research & Practice,* 15(3), pp. 241–7.

2   Ibid. p. 242.

3   Clance, P. R. and Imes, S. A. (1978) The imposter phenomenon in high achieving women: Dynamics and therapeutic intervention. *Psychotherapy: Theory, Research & Practice,* 15(3), pp. 241–7; Bernard, N. S., Dollinger, S. J. and Ramaniah, N. V. (2002) Applying the big five personality factors to the impostor phenomenon. *Journal of Personality Assessment,* 78(2), pp. 321–33; Badawy, R. L., Gazdag, B. A., Bentley, J. R. and Brouer, R. L. (2018) Are all impostors created equal? Exploring gender differences in the impostor phenomenon-performance link. *Personality and Individual Differences,* 131; Want, J. and Kleitman, S. (2006) Imposter phenomenon and self-handicapping: Links with parenting styles and self-confidence. *Personality and Individual Differences,* 40, pp. 961–71.

4   Sandberg, S. (2013) *Lean In: Women, Work, and the Will to Lead.* London: Random House.

5   Obama, M. (2018) *Becoming.* New York: Crown Publishing Group.

6   Arkin, R. M., Oleson, K. C. and Carroll, P. J. (2013) *Handbook of the Uncertain Self.* Hove: Psychology Press.

7   Jöstl, G., Bergsmann, E., Lüftenegger, M., Schober, B. and Spiel, C. (2015) When will they blow my cover? *Zeitschrift für Psychologie,* 220(2), pp. 109–20; McDowell, W. C., Grubb, W. L. and Geho, P. R. (2015) The impact of self-efficacy and perceived organizational support on the imposter phenomenon. *American Journal of Management,* 15(3), pp. 23–9; Pákozdy, C., Askew, J., Dyer, J.,

Gately, P., Martin, L., Mavor, K. I. and Brown, G. R. (2024) The imposter phenomenon and its relationship with self-efficacy, perfectionism and happiness in university students. *Current Psychology*, 43, 5153–62; Want, J. and Kleitman, S. (2006) Imposter phenomenon and self-handicapping: Links with parenting styles and self-confidence. *Personality and Individual Differences*, 40, pp. 961–71.

8 Tao, K. W. and Gloria, A. M. (2018) Should I stay or should I go? The role of impostorism in stem persistence. *Psychology of Women Quarterly*, 43(2), pp. 151–64.

9 Bandura, A. (1977) Self-efficacy: Toward a unifying theory of behavioral change. *Psychological Review*, 84(2), pp. 191–215.

10 Pennebaker, J. W. and Smyth, J. M. (2016) *Opening Up by Writing it Down: How Expressive Writing Improves Health and Eases Emotional Pain.* Guilford Publications.

11 Neff, K. D. (2011) Self-compassion, self-esteem, and well-being. *Social and Personality Psychology Compass*, 5(1), pp. 1–12.

12 Patzak, A., Kollmayer, M. and Schober, B. (2017) Buffering impostor feelings with kindness: The mediating role of self-compassion between gender-role orientation and the impostor phenomenon. *Frontiers in Psychology*, 8.

13 https://www.ted.com/talks/amy_cuddy_your_body_language_may_shape_who_you_are?language=en.

14 Brooks, A. W. (2014) Get excited: Reappraising pre-performance anxiety as excitement. *Journal of Experimental Psychology: General*, 143(3), pp. 1144–58.

Chapter 2

1 Quinn, R. E. and Quinn, G. T. (2002) *Letters to Garrett: Stories of Change, Power, and Possibility.* Hoboken NJ: Jossey-Bass.

2 Rohrmann, S., Bechtoldt, M. and Leonhardt, M. (2016) Validation of the impostor phenomenon among managers. *Frontiers in Psychology*, 7: Article 821; Kaur, T. and Jain, N. (2022) Relationship between impostor phenomenon and

personality traits: A study on undergraduate students. *Journal of Positive School Psychology*, 6(11), pp. 734–46.

3 Clance, P. R. and Imes, S. A. (1978) The imposter phenomenon in high achieving women: Dynamics and therapeutic intervention. *Psychotherapy: Theory, Research & Practice*, 15(3), pp. 241–7.

4 Gravois, J. (2007) You're not fooling anyone. *The Chronicle of Higher Education*, 54(11); Matthews, G. and Clance, P. R. (1985) Treatment of the impostor phenomenon in psychotherapy clients. *Psychotherapy in Private Practice*, 3(1), pp. 71–81.

5 Kruger, J. and Dunning, D. (1999) Unskilled and unaware of it: How difficulties in recognizing one's own incompetence lead to inflated self-assessments. *Journal of Personality and Social Psychology*, 77(6), pp. 1121–34.

6 Rohrmann, S., Bechtoldt, M. and Leonhardt, M. (2016) Validation of the impostor phenomenon among managers. *Frontiers in Psychology*, 7: Article 821; Kaur, T. and Jain, N. (2022) Relationship between impostor phenomenon and personality traits: A study on undergraduate students. *Journal of Positive School Psychology*, 6(11), pp. 734–46.

7 Clance, P. R. and Imes, S. A. (1978) The imposter phenomenon in high achieving women: Dynamics and therapeutic intervention. *Psychotherapy: Theory, Research & Practice*, 15(3), pp. 241–7.

8 Deaux, K. (1976) Sex: A perspective on the attribution process. In Harvey, J. H., Ickes, W. J. and Kidd, R. F. (eds) *New Directions in Attribution Research*. New York: Halsted Press Division, Wiley.

9 Jones, E. E. and Berglas, S. (1978) Control of attributions about the self through self-handicapping strategies: The appeal of alcohol and the role of underachievement. *Personality and Social Psychology Bulletin*, 4(2), pp. 200–206.

10 Hirt, E. R. and McCrea, S. M. (2009) Man smart, woman smarter? Getting to the root of gender differences in self-handicapping. *Social and Personality Psychology Compass*, 3, pp. 260–74.

11 Ibid.

12 Ferrari, J. R. and Thompson, T. (2006) Impostor fears: Links
with self-presentational concerns and self-handicapping behaviours. *Personality and Individual Differences*, 40(2), pp. 341–
52; Cowman, S. E. and Ferrari, J. R. (2002) 'Am I for real?'
Predicting impostor tendencies from self-handicapping and
affective components. *Social Behavior and Personality: an international journal*, 30(2), pp. 119–25.

13 Clance, P. R. and Imes, S. A. (1978) The imposter phenomenon
in high achieving women: Dynamics and therapeutic intervention. *Psychotherapy: Theory, Research & Practice*, 15(3),
pp. 241–7; Clance, P. R. and O'Toole, M. A. (1987) The imposter
phenomenon: An internal barrier to empowerment and achievement. *Women & Therapy*, 6(3), pp. 51–64.

14 Saini, A. (2023) *The Patriarchs: How Men Came to Rule*.
HarperCollins UK.

15 Quadlin, N. (2018) The mark of a woman's record: Gender and
academic performance in hiring. *American Sociological Review*,
83(2), pp. 331–60.

16 Matthews, G. and Clance, P. R. (1985) Treatment of the impostor
phenomenon in psychotherapy clients. *Psychotherapy in Private
Practice*, 3(1), pp. 71–81.

17 Villwock, J. A., Sobin, L. B., Koester, L. A. and Harris, T. M.
(2016) Impostor syndrome and burnout among American medical students: A pilot study. *International Journal of Medical
Education*, 7, p. 364.

18 Dweck, C. (2017) *Mindset – Updated edition: Changing the Way
You Think to Fulfil Your Potential*. London: Hachette UK.

19 Perry, P. (2019) *The Book You Wish Your Parents Had Read (and
Your Children Will Be Glad That You Did)*. London: Penguin UK.

20 Goldberg, L. R. (1990) An alternative "description of personality": The big-five factor structure. *Journal of Personality and
Social Psychology*, 59(6), pp. 1216–1229.

21 Bernard, N. S., Dollinger, S. J. and Ramaniah, N. V. (2002)
Applying the big five personality factors to the impostor phe-
nomenon. *Journal of Personality Assessment*, 78(2), pp. 321–33;
Ross, S. R., Stewart, J., Mugge, M. and Fultz, B. (2001) The

imposter phenomenon, achievement dispositions, and the five factor model. *Personality and Individual Differences*, 31(8), pp. 1347–55.

22 Ross, S. R. and Krukowski, R. A. (2003) The imposter phenomenon and maladaptive personality: Type and trait characteristics. *Personality and Individual Differences*, 34(3), pp. 477–84; Vergauwe, J., Wille, B., Feys, M., De Fruyt, F. and Anseel, F. (2015) Fear of being exposed: The trait-relatedness of the impostor phenomenon and its relevance in the work context. *Journal of Business and Psychology*, 30(3), pp. 565–81.

23 Cokley, K., Smith, L., Bernard, D., Hurst, A., Jackson, S., Stone, S., Awosogba, O., Saucer, C., Bailey, M. and Roberts, D. (2017) Impostor feelings as a moderator and mediator of the relationship between perceived discrimination and mental health among racial/ethnic minority college students. *Journal of Counseling Psychology*, 64(2), pp. 141–54; Bernard, D. L., Hoggard, L. S. and Neblett Jr, E. W. (2018) Racial discrimination, racial identity, and impostor phenomenon: A profile approach. *Cultural Diversity and Ethnic Minority Psychology*, 24(1), pp. 51–62; Peteet, B. J., Montgomery, L. and Weekes, J. C. (2015) Predictors of imposter phenomenon among talented ethnic minority undergraduate students. *The Journal of Negro Education*, 84(2), pp. 175–86; Sivananthajothy, P., Adel, A., Afhami, S., Castrogiovanni, N., Osei-Tutu, K. and Brown, A. (2023) Equity, diversity, and . . . exclusion? A national mixed methods study of 'belonging' in Canadian undergraduate medical education. *Advances in Health Sciences Education*.

24 Vaughn, A. R., Taasoobshirazi, G. and Johnson, M. L. (2019) Impostor phenomenon and motivation: Women in higher education. *Studies in Higher Education*, 45(4), pp. 780–95.

25 https://edu.admin.ox.ac.uk/what-is-edi-and-why-does-it-matter.

26 Nickerson, R.S. (1998) Confirmation bias: A ubiquitous phenomenon in many guises. *Review of General Psychology*, 2(2), pp. 175–220.

27 https://hbr.org/2021/02/stop-telling-women-they-have-imposter-syndrome.

28 Mustafa, F. (2024) To explore the impact of my leadership in developing talent management interventions and strategies to cope with Imposter Syndrome for aspiring Black, Asian and Minority Ethnic senior leaders to better represent the diverse patient population. Unpublished master's thesis. University of Birmingham and University of Manchester.

Chapter 3

1   Bernard, D. L., Lige, Q. M., Willis, H. A., Sosoo, E. E. and Neblett, E. W. (2017) Impostor phenomenon and mental health: The influence of racial discrimination and gender. *Journal of Counseling Psychology*, 64(2), pp. 155–66; Haar, J. and De Jong, K. (2022) Imposter phenomenon and employee mental health: What role do organizations play? *Personnel Review*, 53(1), pp. 211–27; Salicru, S. (2022) A new model to treat impostor syndrome and associated conditions. *American Journal of Applied Psychology*, 11(1), pp. 17–27.

2   https://nypost.com/2023/03/13/catch-me-if-you-can-conman-frank-abagnale-lied-about-his-lies/.

3   Leary, M. R., Patton, K. M., Orlando, A. E. and Wagoner Funk, W. (2000) The impostor phenomenon: Self-perceptions, reflected appraisals, and interpersonal strategies. *Journal of Personality*, 68(4), pp. 725–56; Leonhardt, M., Bechtoldt, M. N. and Rohrmann, S. (2017) All impostors aren't alike – differentiating the impostor phenomenon. *Frontiers in Psychology*, 8.

4   Bernard, D. L., Lige, Q. M., Willis, H. A., Sosoo, E. E. and Neblett, E. W. (2017) Impostor phenomenon and mental health: The influence of racial discrimination and gender. *Journal of Counseling Psychology*, 64(2), pp. 155–66; Haar, J. and De Jong, K. (2022) Imposter phenomenon and employee mental health: What role do organizations play? *Personnel Review*, 53(1), pp. 211–27; Rohrmann, S., Bechtoldt, M. and Leonhardt, M. (2016) Validation of the impostor phenomenon among managers. *Frontiers in Psychology*, 7: Article 821.

5   Bernard, N. S., Dollinger, S. J. and Ramaniah, N. V. (2002)
    Applying the big five personality factors to the impostor
    phenomenon. *Journal of Personality Assessment*, 78(2), pp. 321–33.

Chapter 4

1   Clance, P. R. and O'toole, M. A. (1987) The imposter phenom-
    enon: An internal barrier to empowerment and achievement.
    Women & Therapy, 6(3), pp. 51–64.
2   Burris, E. R. (2012) The risks and rewards of speaking up:
    Managerial responses to employee voice. *Academy of Management
    Journal*, 55(4), pp. 851–75; Sanford, A. A., Ross, E. M., Blake, S. J.
    and Cambiano, R. L. (2015) Finding courage and confirmation:
    Resisting impostor feelings through relationships with mentors,
    romantic partners, and other women in leadership. *Advancing
    Women in Leadership*, 35, pp. 33–43.
3   Dudău, D. P. (2014) The relation between perfectionism and
    impostor phenomenon. *Procedia – Social and Behavioral Sciences*,
    127(2014), pp. 129–33; Vergauwe, J., Wille, B., Feys, M., De Fruyt,
    F. and Anseel, F. (2015) Fear of being exposed: The trait-related-
    ness of the impostor phenomenon and its relevance in the work
    context. *Journal of Business and Psychology*, 30(3), pp. 565–81.
4   https://www.linkedin.com/feed/update/urn:li:activi-
    ty:7202640881932218368/?originTrackingId=B1qpiukmR7Gej-
    d04AC4uZg%3D%3D
5   Hill, E. (2022) Can feeling like an imposter be favorable? A qual-
    itative study on the role of appraisal in harnessing the imposter
    phenomenon for growth. Master's thesis, University of Central
    Florida.
6   Villwock, J. A., Sobin, L.B., Koester, L.A., Harris, T.M. (2016)
    Impostor syndrome and burnout among American medical stu-
    dents: a pilot study. *International Journal of Medical Education*,
    7, 364–9; Stoeber, J. and Damian, L. E. (2016) Perfectionism in
    employees: Work engagement, workaholism, and burnout. In
    Sirois, F. M. and Molnar, D. S. (eds), *Perfectionism, Health, and*

Well-being (pp. 265–83). Springer International Publishing/ Springer Nature; Clark, P., Holden, C., Russell, M., *et al.* (2022) The impostor phenomenon in mental health professionals: Relationships among compassion fatigue, burnout, and compassion satisfaction. *Contemporary Family Therapy*, 44, pp. 185–97.

7   Tewfik, B. (2023) The impostor phenomenon revisited: Examining the relationship between workplace impostor thoughts and interpersonal effectiveness at work. *Academy of Management Journal*, 65, 988–1018.

8   Mitchell, G., McMurray, A. J., Manoharan, A. and Rajesh, J. I. (2024) Workplace and workplace leader arrogance: A conceptual framework. *International Journal of Management Reviews*.

9   Clance, P. R. (1985) *The Impostor Phenomenon: Overcoming the Fear that Haunts your Success*. Atlanta: Peachtree Pub Ltd.

10   September, A. N., Mccarrey, M., Baranowsky, A., Patent, C. and Schindler, D. (2001) The relation between well-being, impostor feelings, and gender role orientation among Canadian university students. *The Journal of Social Psychology*, 141(2), pp. 218–32.

11   Pákozdy, C., Askew, J., Dyer, J., Gately, P., Martin, L., Mavor, K. I. and Brown, G. R. (2024) The imposter phenomenon and its relationship with self-efficacy, perfectionism and happiness in university students. *Current Psychology*, 43, pp. 5153–62.

12   Rohrmann, S., Bechtoldt, M. and Leonhardt, M. (2016) Validation of the impostor phenomenon among managers. *Frontiers in Psychology*, 7: Article 821.

13   Jones, E. E. and Berglas, S. (1978) Control of attributions about the self through self-handicapping strategies: The appeal of alcohol and the role of underachievement. *Personality and Social Psychology Bulletin*, 4(2), pp. 200–6.

14   Curran, T. (2023) *The Perfection Trap: The Power of Good Enough in a World That Always Wants More*. Random House.

15   Cozzarelli, C. and Major, B. (1990) Exploring the validity of the impostor phenomenon. *Journal of Social and Clinical Psychology*, 9(4), pp. 401–17.

16 Dudău, D. P. (2014) The relation between perfectionism and impostor phenomenon. *Procedia – Social and Behavioral Sciences,* 127, pp. 129–33.

17 Cowman, S. E. and Ferrari, J. R. (2002) 'Am I for real?' Predicting impostor tendencies from self-handicapping and affective components. *Social Behavior and Personality: An International Journal,* 30(2), pp. 119–25.

18 Clance, P. R., Dingman, D., Reviere, S. L. and Stober, D. R. (1995) Impostor phenomenon in an interpersonal/social context: Origins and treatment. *Women & Therapy,* 16(4), pp. 79–96.

19 Clance, P. R. and O'Toole, M. A. (1987) The imposter phenomenon: An internal barrier to empowerment and achievement. *Women & Therapy,* 6(3), pp. 51–64.

20 Brown, B. (2022) *The Gifts of Imperfection: Let Go of Who You Think You're Supposed to be and Embrace Who You Are.* Simon and Schuster.

21 Grubb, W. L. and Grubb, L. K. (2021) Perfectionism and the imposter phenomenon. *Journal of Organizational Psychology,* 21(6), pp. 25–42.

22 Hamachek, D. E. (1978) Psychodynamics of normal and neurotic perfectionism. *Psychology: A Journal of Human Behavior,* 15(1), pp. 27–33.

23 Clance, P. R. and O'Toole, M. A. (1987) The Imposter Phenomenon: An internal barrier to empowerment and achievement. *Women & Therapy,* 6(3), pp. 51–64.

Chapter 5

1 Whitman, M. V. and Shanine, K. K. (2012) Revisiting the impostor phenomenon: How individuals cope with feelings of being in over their heads. *The Role of the Economic Crisis on Occupational Stress and Well Being,* 10, pp. 177–12; Kark, R., Meister, A. and Peters, K. (2022) Now you see me, now you don't: A conceptual model of the antecedents and consequences of leader impostorism. *Journal of Management,* 48(7), pp. 1948–79.

2   Bechtoldt, M. N. (2015) Wanted: Self-doubting employees –
    managers scoring positively on impostorism favor insecure
    employees in task delegation. *Personality and Individual
    Differences*, 86, pp. 482–6.

3   Clance, P. R. and O'Toole, M. A. (1987) The imposter phenomenon:
    An internal barrier to empowerment and achievement. *Women &
    Therapy*, 6(3), pp. 51–64.

4   Mcdowell, W. C., Boyd, N. G. and Bowler, W. M. (2007)
    Overreward and the impostor phenomenon. *Journal of
    Managerial Issues*, 19(1), pp. 95–110; Whitman, M. V. and
    Shanine, K. K. (2012) Revisiting the impostor phenomenon:
    How individuals cope with feelings of being in over their heads.
    *The Role of the Economic Crisis on Occupational Stress and Well
    Being*, 10, pp. 177–212.

5   Adams, J. S. (1963) Towards an understanding of inequity. *The
    Journal of Abnormal and Social Psychology*, 67(5), pp. 422–36;
    Adams, J. S. (1965) Inequity in social exchange. *Advances in
    Experimental Social Psychology*. Elsevier.

6   Neureiter, M. and Traut-Mattausch, E. (2016) Inspecting the
    dangers of feeling like a fake: An empirical investigation of
    the impostor phenomenon in the world of work. *Frontiers in
    Psychology*, 7.

7   Lepine, J. A. and Van Dyne, L. (1998) Predicting voice behavior
    in work groups. *Journal of Applied Psychology*, 83(6).

8   Burris, E. R. (2012) The risks and rewards of speaking
    up: Managerial responses to employee voice. *Academy of
    Management Journal*, 55(4), pp. 851–75.

9   Edmondson, A. (2018) *The Fearless Organization: Creating
    Psychological Safety in the Workplace for Learning, Innovation,
    and Growth*. New Jersey: John Wiley & Sons; https://www.ccl.
    org/articles/leading-effectively-articles/what-is-psychological-
    safety-at-work/?utm_campaign=General+awareness&utm_
    content=psychological_safety_is_k&utm_creative_format=Ar-
    ticle,Insight,Preview&utm_medium=social&utm_source=linke-
    din; https://psychsafety.co.uk/googles-project-aristotle/.

10 Chodoff, A., Conyers, L., Wright, S. and Levine, R. (2023) 'I never should have been a doctor': A qualitative study of imposter phenomenon among internal medicine residents. *BMC Medical Education*, 23.

11 Clance, P. R. and Imes, S. A. (1978) The imposter phenomenon in high achieving women: Dynamics and therapeutic intervention. *Psychotherapy: Theory, Research & Practice*, 15(3), pp. 241–7.

12 Gadsby, S. and Hohwy, J. (2024) Negative performance evaluation in the imposter phenomenon. *Current Psychology*, 43, pp. 9300–8.

13 Burris, E. R. (2012) The risks and rewards of speaking up: Managerial responses to employee voice. *Academy of Management Journal*, 55(4), pp. 851–75.

14 Detert, J. R. and Burris, E. R. (2007) Leadership behavior and employee voice: Is the door really open? *Academy of Management Journal*, 50(4), pp. 869–84.

15 https://www.ted.com/talks/charlie_mackesy_abandon_the_idea_of_being_good_and_just_try?subtitle=en.

16 Janis, I. L. (1982) *Groupthink: Psychological Studies of Policy Decisions and Fiascoes*. Boston: Houghton Mifflin; https://www.pbs.org/independentlens/blog/psychology-of-groupthink-desperate-dangerous-desire-for-social-acceptance/.

Chapter 6

1 https://www.youtube.com/watch?v=ZQUxL4Jm1Lo&t=3s.

2 Mackesy, C. (2019) *The Boy, the Mole, the Fox and the Horse. Ebury Press*. Penguin Random House

3 Sanford, A. A., Ross, E. M., Blake, S. J. and Cambiano, R. L. (2015) Finding courage and confirmation: Resisting impostor feelings through relationships with mentors, romantic partners, and other women in leadership. *Advancing Women in Leadership*, 35, pp. 33–43; Vergauwe, J., Wille, B., Feys, M., De Fruyt, F. and Anseel, F. (2015) Fear of being exposed: The trait-relatedness of

the impostor phenomenon and its relevance in the work context. *Journal of Business and Psychology*, 30(3), pp. 565–81.

4 Haar, J. and De Jong, K. (2022) Imposter phenomenon and employee mental health: What role do organizations play? *Personnel Review*, 53(1), pp. 211–27.

5 Finfgeld, D. L. (1999) Courage as a process of pushing beyond the struggle. *Qualitative Health Research*, 9(6), pp. 803–14.

6 Sanford, A. A., Ross, E. M., Blake, S. J. and Cambiano, R. L. (2015) Finding courage and confirmation: Resisting impostor feelings through relationships with mentors, romantic partners, and other women in leadership. *Advancing Women in Leadership*, 35, pp. 33–43.

7 Kirton, G. and Greene, A. (2015) *The Dynamics of Managing Diversity and Inclusion: A Critical Approach*. London: Routledge.

8 Hutchins, H. M. and Rainbolt, H. (2017) What triggers imposter phenomenon among academic faculty? A critical incident study exploring antecedents, coping, and development opportunities. *Human Resource Development International*, 20(3), pp. 194–214; Lane, J. A. (2015) The imposter phenomenon among emerging adults transitioning into professional life: Developing a grounded theory. *Adultspan Journal*, 14(2), pp. 114–28.

9 Arkin, R. M., Oleson, K. C. and Carroll, P. J. (2013) *Handbook of the Uncertain Self*. Hove: Psychology Press.

10 https://www.youtube.com/watch?v=NSEHo90QLLs.

11 Dudău, D. P. (2014) The relation between perfectionism and impostor phenomenon. *Procedia – Social and Behavioral Sciences*, 127, pp. 129–33; Vergauwe, J., Wille, B., Feys, M., De Fruyt, F. and Anseel, F. (2015) Fear of being exposed: The trait-relatedness of the impostor phenomenon and its relevance in the work context. *Journal of Business and Psychology*, 30(3), pp. 565–81.

12 Hobfoll, S. E. (1989) Conservation of resources: A new attempt at conceptualizing stress. *American Psychologist*, 44(3), pp. 513–24; Mcgarry, T., Stevens, M. and Eme-Power, J. (2022). The clandestine cost of feeling like a fake: Imposter phenomenon and workplace presenteeism. *Academy of Management Proceedings*, 2022, 14762.

13 Leonard, N. H. and Harvey, M. (2008) Negative perfectionism: Examining negative excessive behavior in the workplace. *Journal of Applied Social Psychology*, 38(3), pp. 585–610; Pannhausen, S., Klug, K. and Rohrmann, S. (2022) Never good enough: The relation between the imposter phenomenon and multidimensional perfectionism. *Current Psychology*, 41, pp. 888–901.

14 Villwock, J. A., Sobin, L. B., Koester, L. A. and Harris, T. M. (2016) Impostor syndrome and burnout among American medical students: A pilot study. *International Journal of Medical Education*, 7, p. 364; Stoeber, J. and Damian, L. E. (2016) Perfectionism in employees: Work engagement, workaholism, and burnout. In Sirois, F. M. and Molnar, D. S. (eds) *Perfectionism, Health, and Well-being*. New York: Springer.

15 Ben-Shahar, T. (2009) *The Pursuit of Perfect*. New York: McGraw Hill.

16 Norem, J. K. and Chang, E. C. (2002) The positive psychology of negative thinking. *Journal of Clinical Psychology*, 58(9), pp. 993–1001.

17 Plato (1987) *Laches*. Translated by Nichols Jr, J. Ithaca: Cornell University Press.

18 Tillich, P. (2000) *The Courage To Be*. Second edition. New Haven, CT: Yale University Press.

19 Baum, L. F. (1900) *The Wonderful Wizard of Oz*. New York: George M. Hill Company.

20 Hannah, S. T., Sweeney, P. J. and Lester, P. B. (2007) Toward a courageous mindset: The subjective act and experience of courage. *The Journal of Positive Psychology*, 2(2), pp. 129–35.

21 Putman, D. A. (2004) *Psychological Courage*. Maryland: University Press of America.

22 Peterson, C. and Seligman, M. E. P. (2004) *Character Strengths and Virtues: A Handbook and Classification*. New York: Oxford University Press; https://www.viacharacter.org/account/register.

23 Pury, C. L. S. and Kowalski, R. M. (2007) Human strengths, cou-
    rageous actions, and general and personal courage. *The Journal
    of Positive Psychology*, 2(2), pp. 120–8.
24 Hannah, S. T., Sweeney, P. J. and Lester, P. B. (2007) Toward a
    courageous mindset: The subjective act and experience of cour-
    age. *The Journal of Positive Psychology*, 2(2), pp. 129–35.

Chapter 7

1   Thompson, T., Foreman, P. and Martin, F. (2000) Impostor
    fears and perfectionistic concern over mistakes. *Personality and
    Individual Differences*, 29(4), pp. 629–47; Grubb, W. L. and Grubb, L.
    K. (2021) Perfectionism and the imposter phenomenon. *Journal
    of Organizational Psychology*, 21(6), pp. 25–42.
2   Thompson, T., Davis, H. and Davidson, J. (1998) Attributional
    and affective responses of impostors to academic success and
    failure outcomes. *Personality and Individual Differences*, 25(2),
    pp. 381–96.
3   Lane, J. A. (2015) The imposter phenomenon among emerg-
    ing adults transitioning into professional life: Developing a
    grounded theory. *Adultspan Journal*, 14(2), pp. 114–28.
4   Gravois, J. (2007) You're not fooling anyone. *The Chronicle of
    Higher Education*, 54(11); Matthews, G. and Clance, P. R. (1985)
    Treatment of the impostor phenomenon in psychotherapy
    clients. *Psychotherapy in Private Practice*, 3(1), pp. 71–81.
5   Carson, R. D. (1983) *Taming your Gremlin: A Guide to Enjoying
    Yourself.* Perennial Library.
6   Vergauwe, J., Wille, B., Feys, M., De Fruyt, F. and Anseel, F.
    (2015) Fear of being exposed: The trait-relatedness of the impos-
    tor phenomenon and its relevance in the work context. *Journal
    of Business and Psychology*, 30(3), pp. 565–81; Kaur, T. and Jain,
    N. (2022) Relationship between impostor phenomenon and per-
    sonality traits: A study on undergraduate students. *Journal of
    Positive School Psychology*, 6(11), pp. 734–46.

7 Kaufman , S. B. (2018) Are narcissists more likely to experience impostor syndrome? The surprising link between narcissism and impostor syndrome. Available from: https://blogs.scientificamerican.com/beautiful-minds/ are-narcissists-more-likely-to-experience-impostor-syndrome/.

8 https://www.aatcomment.org.uk/aatpowerup/ how-to-make-your-voice-heard-at-work/.

9 Clance, P. R. and Imes, S. A. (1978) The imposter phenomenon in high achieving women: Dynamics and therapeutic intervention. *Psychotherapy: Theory, Research & Practice*, 15(3), pp. 241–7.

10 Kumar, S. and Jagacinski, C. M. (2006) Imposters have goals too: The imposter phenomenon and its relationship to achievement goal theory. *Personality and Individual Differences*, 40(1), pp. 147–57.

11 Ben-Shahar, T. (2009) *The Pursuit of Perfect*. McGraw Hill.

12 *The Oxford English Dictionary*, s.v. 'optimal (adj.)', July 2023, https://doi.org/10.1093/OED/1089148459.

13 Luthans F. (2002) Positive organizational behavior: Developing and managing psychological strengths. *Academy of Management Executive*, 16(1): 57–72.

14 Brauer, K. and Proyer, R. T. (2017) Are impostors playful? Testing the association of adult playfulness with the impostor phenomenon. *Personality and Individual Differences*, 116, pp. 57–62.

15 Barnett, L. A. (2012) Playful people: Fun is in the mind of the beholder. *Imagination, Cognition and Personality*, 31(3), pp. 169–97.

16 Aaker, J. and Bagdonas, N. (2020) *Humour, Seriously: Why Humour is a Superpower at Work and in Life*. Penguin UK.

17 Youssef, C. M. and Luthans, F. (2007) Positive organizational behavior in the workplace: The impact of hope, optimism, and resilience. *Journal of Management*, 33(5), pp. 774–800.

18 Neff, K. (2003) Self-compassion: An alternative conceptualiza-
    tion of a healthy attitude toward oneself. *Self and Identity*, 2(2),
    pp. 85–101.

19 Kristin Neff speaking on the three components of self-compassion:
    https://www.youtube.com/watch?v=11U0h0DPu7k.

20 Patzak, A., Kollmayer, M. and Schober, B. (2017) Buffering
    impostor feelings with kindness: The mediating role of
    self-compassion between gender-role orientation and the
    impostor phenomenon. *Frontiers in Psychology*, 8, p. 1289.

21 This song is an example of a loving-kindness mantra: https://
    www.youtube.com/watch?v=7YGaumwvKyM.

22 Hutchins, H. M. and Rainbolt, H. (2017) What triggers
    imposter phenomenon among academic faculty? A critical inci-
    dent study exploring antecedents, coping, and development
    opportunities. *Human Resource Development International*,
    20(3), pp. 194–214.

23 McCrea, S. M. and Flamm, A. (2012) Dysfunctional anticipatory
    thoughts and the self-handicapping strategy. *European Journal of
    Social Psychology*, 42(1), pp. 72–81.

24 https://www.youtube.com/watch?v=moSFlvxnbgk.

25 Tao, K. W. and Gloria, A. M. (2018) Should I stay or should
    I go? The role of impostorism in stem persistence. *Psychology of
    Women Quarterly*, 43(2), pp. 151–64.

26 Bandura, A. (1977) Self-efficacy: Toward a unifying the-
    ory of behavioral change. *Psychological Review*, 84(2),
    pp. 191–215.

27 Atkin, K. (2015) *The Confident Manager: Lessons in Confidence
    and Communication for Successful Managers*. SRA Books.

28 Clance, P. R. and Imes, S. A. (1978) The imposter phenomenon in
    high achieving women: Dynamics and therapeutic intervention.
    Psychotherapy: Theory, Research & Practice, 15(3), pp. 241–7.

29 Baumeister, R. F., Bratslavsky, E., Finkenauer, C. and Vohs, K. D.
    (2001) Bad is stronger than good. *Review of General Psychology*,
    5(4), pp. 323–70.

30 https://impro.org.uk/how-a-yes-and-leads-to-more-with-less/.

31 Clance, P. R. and O'Toole, M. A. (1987) The imposter phenomenon: An internal barrier to empowerment and achievement.
Women & Therapy, 6(3), pp. 51–64.

32 Linley, P. A., Nielsen, K. M., Gillett, R. and Biswas-Diener, R.
(2010). Using signature strengths in pursuit of goals: Effects
on goal progress, need satisfaction, and well-being, and impli-
cations for coaching psychologists. *International Coaching
Psychology Review*, 5(1), pp. 6–15.

33 https://www.strengthsprofile.com/en-gb/products/free.

34 Linley, P.A. (2008) *Average to A+: Realising Strengths in Yourself
and Others*. CAPP Press.

35 https://cappfinity.com/.

Chapter 8

1 https://www.bbc.com/sport/football/articles/c25ljqrq2w1o.

2 Lopez, S. J. (2007) Profiling courage: Introduction to the special
issue on courage. *The Journal of Positive Psychology*, 2(2), p. 79;
Rachman, S. J. (1984) Fear and courage. *Behavior therapy*, 15(1),
pp. 109–20.

3 Biswas-Diener, R. (2012) *The Courage Quotient: How Science can
Make you Braver*. San Francisco: John Wiley & Sons.

4 Putman, D. A. (2004) *Psychological Courage*. Maryland:
University Press of America.

5 Ibid.

6 Gilbert, P. (2009) *The Compassionate Mind*. London: Constable &
Robinson Ltd.

7 Atkin, K. (2024) How do individuals cope at work in the context
of the Imposter Phenomenon? A thematic analysis study. Anglia
Ruskin Research Online (ARRO). Thesis. https://doi
.org/10.25411/aru.27325224.v1.

8 Brown, B. (2017) *Rising Strong: How the Ability to Reset
Transforms the Way we Live, Love, arent, and Lead*. Random
House.

9 Putman, D. A. (1987) Virtue and self-deception. *The Southern Journal of Philosophy*, 25(4), pp. 549–57.

10 Bandura, A. (1997) *Self-efficacy: The Exercise of Control*. New York: W.H. Freeman.

11 Luft, J. and Ingham, H. (1961) The Johari window. *Human Relations Training News*, 5(1), pp. 6–7.

12 Bandura, A. (1997) *Self-efficacy: The Exercise of Control*. New York: W.H. Freeman, p. 78.

13 Roberts, L. M., Dutton, J. E., Spreitzer, G. M., Heaphy, E. D. and Quinn, R. E. (2005) Composing the reflected best-self portrait: Building pathways for becoming extraordinary in work organizations. *Academy of Management Review*, 30(4), pp. 712–36.

14 Sutcliffe, K. M. and Christianson, M. K. (2012) Managing the unexpected. In Cameron, K. S. and Spreitzer, G. M. (eds) *The Oxford Handbook of Positive Organizational Scholarship*. New York: Oxford University Press.

15 Baumeister, R. F., Bratslavsky, E., Finkenauer, C. and Vohs, K. D. (2001) Bad is stronger than good. *Review of General Psychology*, 5(4), pp. 323–70.

16 Weick, K., Sutcliffe, K. and Obstfeld, D. (2009) Organizing and the process of sensemaking. In Weick, K. E. (ed.) *Making Sense of the Organization: The Impermanent Organization*. Chichester: Wiley.

17 Niemiec, R. (2020) Six functions of character strengths for thriving at times of adversity and opportunity: A theoretical perspective. *Applied Research in Quality of Life*, 15(2), pp. 551–72.

18 Bandura, A. (1977) Self-efficacy: Toward a unifying theory of behavioral change. *Psychological Review*, 84(2), pp. 191–215.

19 https://www.rozsavage.com/the-art-of-courageous-living-week-1-what-is-courage/.

Chapter 9

1 https://www.bbc.co.uk/iplayer/episode/m001llpy/amol-rajan-interviews-richard-branson.

2 Clance, P. R. and Imes, S. A. (1978) The imposter phenomenon in high achieving women: Dynamics and therapeutic intervention. *Psychotherapy: Theory, Research & Practice*, 15(3), pp. 241–7.

3 Cowman, S. E. and Ferrari, J. R. (2002) 'Am I for real?' Predicting imposter tendencies from self-handicapping and affective components. *Social Behavior and Personality: An International Journal*, 30(2), pp. 119–26; Want, J. and Kleitman, S. (2006) Imposter phenomenon and self-handicapping: Links with parenting styles and self-confidence. *Personality and Individual Differences*, 40(5), pp. 961–71; Thompson, T., Davis, H. and Davidson, J. (1998) Attributional and affective responses of impostors to academic success and failure outcomes. *Personality and Individual Differences*, 25(2), pp. 381–96; Rohrmann, S., Bechtoldt, M. N. and Leonhardt, M. (2016) Validation of the impostor phenomenon among managers. *Frontiers in Psychology*, 7, Article 821.

4 Crawford, W. S., Shanine, K. K., Whitman, M. V. and Kacmar, K. M. (2016) Examining the impostor phenomenon and work-family conflict. *Journal of Managerial Psychology*, 31(2), pp. 375–90; Detert, J. R. and Burris, E. R. (2007) Leadership behavior and employee voice: Is the door really open? *Academy of Management Journal*, 50(4), pp. 869–84; Haar, J. and De Jong, K. (2022) Imposter phenomenon and employee mental health: What role do organizations play? *Personnel Review*, 53(1), pp. 211–27.

5 Chodoff, A., Conyers, L., Wright, S. and Levine, R. (2023) 'I never should have been a doctor': A qualitative study of imposter phenomenon among internal medicine residents. *BMC Medical Education*, 23.

6 Brummelman, E., Thomaes, S., Orobio de Castro, B., Overbeek, G. and Bushman, B. J. (2014) The adverse impact of inflated praise on children with low self-esteem. *Psychological Science*, 25(3), pp. 728–35.

7 https://www.toastmasters.org/.

8 Whitman, M. V. and Shanine, K. K. (2012) Revisiting the impostor phenomenon: How individuals cope with feelings of being in over their heads. *The Role of the Economic Crisis on Occupational Stress and Well Being*, 10, pp. 177–212.

9 Fredrickson, B. L. (2001) The role of positive emotions in positive psychology: The broaden-and-build theory of positive emotions. *American Psychologist*, 56(3), pp. 218–26.

10 Gadsby, S. and Hohwy, J. (2024) Negative performance evaluation in the imposter phenomenon. *Current Psychology*, 43, pp. 9300–8.

11 Gardner, R. G., Bednar, J. S., Stewart, B. W., Oldroyd, J. B. and Moore, J. (2019) 'I must have slipped through the cracks somehow': An examination of coping with perceived impostorism and the role of social support. *Journal of Vocational Behavior*.

12 Bravata, D. M., Watts, S. A., Keefer, A. L., Madhusudhan, D. K., Taylor, K. T., Clark, D. M., Nelson, R. S., Cokley, K. O. and Hagg, H. K. (2019) Prevalence, predictors, and treatment of impostor syndrome: A systematic review. *Journal of General Internal Medicine*, 35(4), pp. 1252–75.

13 https://psnet.ahrq.gov/perspective/errors-and-near-misses-what-health-care-could-learn-aviation.

14 Hutchins, H. M., Penney, L. M. and Sublett, L. W. (2017) What imposters risk at work: Exploring imposter phenomenon, stress coping, and job outcomes. *Human Resource Development Quarterly*, 29(1), pp. 31–48; Zanchetta, M., Junker, S., Wolf, A.-M. and Traut-Mattausch, E. (2020) 'Overcoming the fear that haunts your success' – the effectiveness of interventions for reducing the impostor phenomenon. *Frontiers in Psychology*.

15 Christianson, M. K. (2009) Updating as part of everyday work: An interactional perspective. PhD thesis, University of Michigan.

16 https://dictionary.cambridge.org/dictionary/english/reflexivity.

17 Mercier, H. and Sperber, D. eds (2017) *The Enigma of Reason.* Harvard University Press.

18 https://en.wikipedia.org/wiki/World_Kindness_Day.

19 https://www.iso.org/obp/ui/#iso:std:iso:45003:ed-1:v1:en.

Index